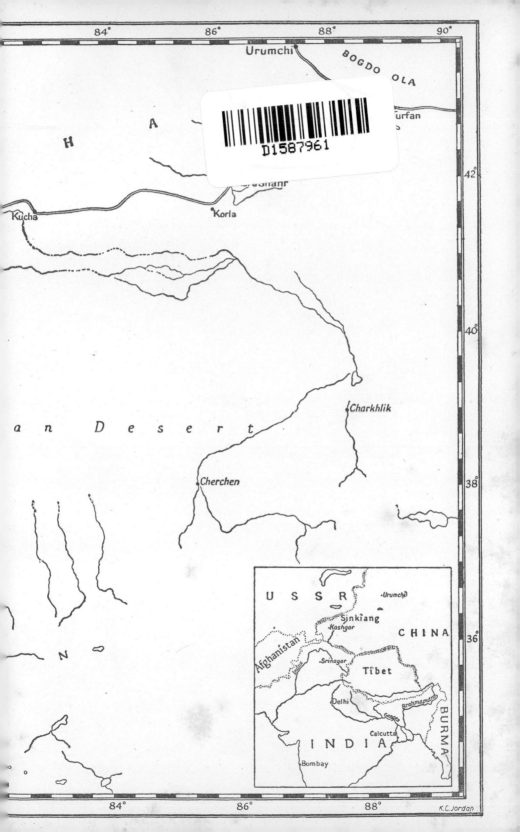

MOUNTAINS *of* TARTARY

KARAKORAM JOURNEY

MOUNTAINS *of* TARTARY

ERIC SHIPTON

Photographs by the Author

LONDON
HODDER AND STOUGHTON

MADE AND PRINTED IN GREAT BRITAIN FOR
HODDER AND STOUGHTON LTD., LONDON, BY
HAZELL, WATSON AND VINEY LTD., AYLESBURY AND LONDON

CONTENTS

ILLUSTRATIONS

7

CHAPTER I

INTRODUCTORY

I WAS returning to Kashgar after a week-end in the mountains, hunting ibex. I had spent Sunday night by a spring
in the foot-hills twenty-five miles to the north-west, and
had started alone just before dawn. My pony knew the
track well and set off at a brisk trot, though I could see
nothing but the outline of the cliffs above me, black against
the stars. With the first grey light he broke into a rhythmic
canter, which he kept up for an hour or more. The wind
was keen against my face; but I was very sleepy and a bit
stiff after the exertions of the previous day. The steep sides
of the valley paled to a ghostly hue. They were utterly
barren; riven and pitted by dark, cavernous nullahs. The
clatter of the pony's hooves echoed hollow, as though it
were the only sound that had ever disturbed the silence of
this dead world.

At a sharp turn the valley ended abruptly, and we
emerged upon flat desert, sloping gently to the great plain.
This was flooded in deep purple shadow; the desert
appeared to sink beneath it, like a shore beneath a lake.
Beyond and above the purple shadow, near or infinitely far
I could not tell, stood the great ice-mountains: the rounded
dome of Kungur, the twin spires of Chakragil, the granite
peaks of Bostan Terek, and scores more unnamed. They were
very white and sharp against the light-blue sky, from which
the stars had lately faded. Sleep and stiffness were swept
away in a sudden wave of ecstasy. I urged the pony to a
gallop. As we raced along, the ice-mountains, one after
another along their huge arc, flushed pink and then kindled
to a burning gold. Gradually, as the rays of the rising sun
struck across it, the purple shadow dissolved, and from it

emerged, first a small group of poplars, then what seemed
to be a dark forest beyond.

At the edge of the oasis my pony drew up, his coat steaming. The Turki inn-keeper came out to greet us. It had
become quite a regular practice, my arrival at his tiny inn
early on Monday morning. He had tea ready and some
bundles of dried lucerne for my pony. A carpet was already
spread for me on the mud floor of the verandah, where half
a dozen other travellers lay asleep, wrapped in their padded
coats. My host woke them with his chatter, and they stared
at me, first with sleepy petulance, then with round-eyed
curiosity. They obviously thought I was Russian. The inn-
keeper soon put them wise.

I paid my host a paltry 40,000 Chinese dollars. My pony
was led reluctantly from his unfinished meal and we trotted
on across the river. We had still another twelve miles to go.
The sun was now well up. The fields of young rice sparkled
in its slanting rays. It was all so green. Thick clusters of
wild iris lined the path. The peasants were already at work.
Judging by their raucous songs, they seemed to find life as
exhilarating as I did. Soon we reached a broad, dusty highway, flanked by willows and poplars. Here I had plenty of
company. But the riders going my way were in no hurry,
and, as I sped by, we had time for no more than a brief
greeting: "*Salaam Alaikum, yakshi kelde ma?*" At intervals
along the road there were villages with stalls laden with
small brown loaves or melons. On we went, past a Chinese
barracks with a guard outside, past an ancient milestone
in the form of a great mud pyramid, along the edge of
a high loess cliff overlooking a marsh, where, in the winter,
I used to go for snipe, till at length the great walls of Kashgar appeared through the trees. At half-past eight we entered
the Consulate compound, in nice time for breakfast, for
which I was more than ready.

That is one of the most characteristic of my memories of

Kashgar; at least so far as the country itself is concerned. There were, of course, other aspects of my life during the four years that I spent there; but this book is not concerned with these. It deals mostly with visits to some of the various mountain ranges surrounding the Tarim Basin.

I discovered long ago that there are many ways of enjoying mountain country. Not even the most enthusiastic Alpine mountaineer would claim that climbing difficult ridges and faces is the only one. Certainly to the critics who denounce his sport as a vulgar display of a useless and artificial skill on a sort of glorified greasy pole, he can with justice reply that mountaineering provides an understanding of mountains and a variety of æsthetic and emotional experience without which he could never achieve a full appreciation of his environment. Experience of a more sombre kind is found in the struggle to reach the summit of a great Himalayan peak; it is unique, perhaps, and certainly well worth while, but so circumscribed that, in my view, a little goes a long way. Mountain exploration, on the other hand, offers limitless scope, and is without doubt the most fascinating occupation I know.

But there is much to be said for a simple mountain journey, whose object, unencumbered with the burden of detailed map-making or scientific observation, is just to get from one place to another. Central Asia provides, *par excellence,* the type of country for journeys of this kind and, of all our little expeditions from Kashgar, I enjoyed these the most. Though many of them were over ground already covered by Stein and Hedin and other travellers, it was easy, even at a week-end, to penetrate unexplored country. Unfortunately, such journeys, however rewarding in themselves, are much harder to describe than quests of discovery or conquest. For, in the absence of any climax or special adventure, unless the writer happens to be a Stevenson or a Doughty, a monotonous repetition of scenic eulogy is apt to result from his efforts to convey his enjoyment, or long and even more boring descriptions of topographical detail from the necessity of presenting some sort of coherent narrative.

For this reason I have been tempted to give undue prominence to the few mountain-climbing ventures in which I indulged, at the expense of the straightforward journeys which were more typical of my contact with those mountain ranges. In the main, these climbing ventures were unsuccessful. This was due largely to bad management and lack of recent practice, partly to bad luck, but mainly to lack of adequate time for reconnaissance, acclimatization and preparation on the spot; for great mountains, however simple, do not readily yield to the first impetuous rush. But the climbs were no less enjoyable for their lack of success—or so I like to think.

It was not my intention to discuss the history, the social and economic life, or the political problems of the country. I have, however, with some misgivings, included one short chapter designed to explain the political background to my experiences. To those who, like myself, are profoundly bored with the politics of a remote land, I recommend skipping that chapter.

Some of the chapters were written while I was still in Kashgar, the rest in moments of ennui and nostalgic recollection, a long time later and in the very different environment of Yunnan.

CHAPTER II

HUNZA—KASHGAR—TASHKENT

I

IN 1937, with two companions, I had spent several months exploring some thousands of square miles of country on the undemarcated frontier of China and India, on the northern side of the Karakoram. It was my first acquaintance with that vast land of mountain-desert and mountain-oasis, so utterly different in form and scale from the parts of the Himalaya that I had visited. As is usually the case in detailed exploration among great mountains, the scope of our travel was severely limited—in time by the seasons, in distance by the labour of moving unaided by animal transport over steep and difficult country. After the months of toil that had gone into its making, our map, when printed on a scale of 1 inch=4 miles, seemed ridiculously small in relation to the stupendous mountain vistas I remembered, an absurdly simple solution to the topographical problems we had puzzled over for so long. But, better than any diary, any album full of photographs, it had the power to re-create in imagination every phase of the experience.

As I look at it now I can recall vividly the feelings with which, during the whole of that summer, I gazed northward to the barren mountains of the Kuen Lun, which for us represented an impossible barrier to an intriguing and very desirable land. Even if the flooding of the Shaksgam had not threatened to cut off our retreat, we could not have travelled beyond the uninhabited regions of the Aghil Range without the certainty of being captured and thrown into a Chinese prison. For at that time Sinkiang was more inaccessible to the Western traveller than it had been for half a century, more inaccessible than Tibet, and scarcely less so than Outer Mongolia. And it seemed, by the way affairs were shaping in Central Asia, that the Iron Curtain had been dropped beyond the Karakoram finally and for ever. Like small boys gazing over a fence into a forbidden park, this rigid political barrier greatly enhanced the enchantment of the remote country, where, compared with the small compass of our horizon, distances were prodigious and where vast areas were still unexplored. I came to regard Sinkiang as one of those places where I could travel only in imagination. Had I been told then that for four years its strange landscape was to become as familiar to me as England, I should have dismissed the notion as fantastic.

But three years later, when, with the outbreak of war, I had abandoned all hope of ever again going to Central Asia, when I was applying my mind, with little success, to learning to be an army officer, I was suddenly taken out of that environment and, in August 1940, sent to Kashgar as Consul-General. In those days one had grown accustomed to refrain from looking far ahead. The fact that the Consulate had for the past couple of years suffered frequent and prolonged boycott; that British subjects (Indian traders) had been suffering severe and calculated maltreatment; that I could hardly expect a pleasant time and would certainly not be free to travel; the strong possibility that Russia, whose influence in that remote spot was then paramount, would enter the war against us—none of these considerations did much to damp my enthusiasm at the prospect of six weeks' trek through the Karakoram, across the great Asiatic watershed and over the Pamirs to the Tarim Basin beyond.

The first half of the journey, from Srinagar to Gilgit and through the Hunza gorges for ten marches beyond, I already knew well. But I could never have enough of it. Hunza is the most spectacular country I have ever seen. For a hundred and fifty miles the caravan route follows along the great gorge of the Hunza River, through the very heart of the greatest concentration of high mountains in the

BALTIT, CAPITAL OF HUNZA

KASHGAR : FLOUR MILL

world. The whole way the river is closely flanked by peaks more than twenty thousand feet high. The first of the giants is Rakaposhi, whose northern face rises straight out of the river-bed at 6,000 feet, first through forested slopes, up steep glacier corries to the great ice-buttresses which support its lovely snow summit (25,550 feet), nearly twenty thousand feet above. A large part of the caravan road is carved out of the sheer sides of the gorge, but every few miles there is a village oasis of terraced fields, fruit trees, briars, willows and poplars, vivid green in spring and summer, aflame with red and gold in autumn. Where the gorge widens out around Baltit, the capital, these villages merge into a great area of intensive cultivation, perhaps forty square miles in extent. Above stand the vast rock walls of the Kanjut Peaks, whose summits, individually unnamed, rise to 24,000 feet. It is difficult to describe this fantastic principality without indulging in superlatives. Both to look at and in character the people are worthy of the unique setting of their country. We like to romanticize about mountain people; and certainly some have produced as fine types as can be found anywhere. But they are so often marred by a high proportion of goitred and cretinous people. The Hunzas are remarkably free from this affliction. Indeed, I have heard it said that there is less sickness, disease and malformity in Hunza in proportion to the size of the population than anywhere else on earth. Their passion for polo is evidence of their splendid horsemanship; as natural mountaineers it would be hard to find their peers. They are proud, loyal, brave and open-hearted. They certainly lack subtlety, but they are not less likeable for that.

My caravan was a large one, for besides the ponies carrying my own baggage and stores for two years, two Indian clerks were travelling with me. I had brought as servants two Sherpas, Lhakpa Tenzing and Rinzing, who had been with me on several Himalayan expeditions. We crossed the Mintaka Pass (15,600 feet), on the frontier, in a snowstorm. Beyond the pass the country changed sud-

denly and completely. The great gorges and huge mountains
of the Karakoram gave place to rounded hills and grassy,
U-shaped valleys, with only a few, comparatively small
glaciated peaks. We spent our first night in Sinkiang, un-
molested, in the pleasant valley at the northern foot
of the pass. The next morning, after we had gone a few
miles down the valley, we met a platoon of mounted Chinese
soldiers under the charge of a young officer. The latter was
quite polite, but he told me that we must halt where we were.
I showed him our papers, which, of course, included diplomatic visas issued by the Chinese Consul-General in Calcutta. However, these did not interest him much and he said
we must wait until he got permission from higher authority
to let us through. I asked how long this would take and he
replied that he hoped to get a reply within a week. We spent
most of the rest of the day arguing the toss. But it was quite
useless, and, wondering how far I would be allowed to
explore the surrounding mountains, I resigned myself to a
long wait.

However, the officer evidently reconsidered his decision
overnight and early the next morning he informed us that we
were to proceed with an armed escort. We marched for thirty
miles and as it was getting dark we reached the wide open
valley known as the Taghdumbash Pamir. We started again
very early the next morning, but before we had gone more
than five miles we reached a large, gaunt fort at a place called
Dafdar. We were ordered to halt half a mile from the fort
and told not to move until we received further instructions.
I expected the commander of the garrison to come out to see
me, or at least to be summoned to his presence. But we
waited all day in vain, and towards evening we pitched camp.
The next morning I rode over to the fort with the intention
of paying a call, and finding out the form. As I approached
the great mud walls and the large, six-pointed red star
painted over the entrance, three soldiers appeared on top of
the parapet and waved me back. At first I took no notice and

continued riding towards the entrance. The soldiers shouted angrily and finally aimed their rifles at me. I took this gentle hint and returned to camp. In spite of this depressing treatment, I found infinite satisfaction in being in this strange and beautiful land. Far away to the north I could see the great ice-dome of Mustagh Ata. Some fine granite peaks flanked the wide valley on the west. The great distances, the clear, cold air, the intense blue of the sky, the bare, rounded hills that coloured so vividly in the evening light— it all reminded me very much of the plateau of Tibet.

On the third day two officers and some soldiers came over to our camp, made a thorough search of our baggage, making us open all our cases of stores, and told us to be ready to start early the following morning. With another armed escort we marched thirty-five miles and arrived at Tash-kurghan late in the evening. We were herded into a filthy serai, pack-ponies and all, and an armed guard placed at the entrance to see that none of us emerged. There we were kept for another three days. We were not allowed out for any purpose, except to answer calls of nature, and then we were escorted by one of the sentries, presumably to check that our stated reason was genuine. I requested permission to call on the local magistrate, but this was ignored. Eventually one morning a number of policemen with red stars in their caps turned up and started to search our belongings. I had thought that the examination at Dafdar had been thorough, but it was a mere cursory glance compared with this. All the boxes of stores had, of course, to be opened again; all garments were turned inside out and linings were felt with the utmost care; the clothes we were wearing were subjected to an equally rigorous search; a statement of my bank account was studied minutely (at least that was in the right colour!). Whatever was the nature of the contraband that they hoped to find, it must have been capable of being carried in extremely small pieces—opium, perhaps, or vile imperialist propaganda in tabloid form. I had with me a simple route-map. This was taken to be studied, presumably by higher and more expert authorities. Fortunately, none of the party had brought with him any of the incriminating articles so diligently sought, and on the following morning we were told that we could proceed with our journey to Kashgar.

All this was not quite the kind of welcome that might reasonably be expected by the accredited representative of a friendly country. But I was not at all surprised, though it served as a salutary reminder of the kind of treatment that we could look for during our stay in Kashgar. It was clearly not worth raising any objections then, and though I submitted a formal protest when I reached Kashgar, I did not receive, nor did I expect, any apology. The Indians, Sirdar Raza Ali and Qazi Gulam Sarwar, behaved with admirable restraint and good-humour, which won my lasting regard and was a great encouragement for the future.

It was a wonderful relief to be on the move again. To my amazement I found that no armed guard had been attached to our party. For some time I expected to see mounted policemen or soldiers chasing after us. But when we left the wide valley of the Taghdumbash and made our way up the narrow little gorge into the mountains of the Kungur-Mustagh Ata massif, I felt sure that I was to be left in peace and freedom to enjoy the last ten days of the journey. Wanting to get as far as possible from the unpleasant memory of Tashkurghan, we made a long march that day, in spite of a fairly late start. It was evening when we reached the 13,500-foot Chichilik Pass, which has two summits, with a wide, undulating plateau between. This was already deep in snow. I was riding alone, well ahead of the caravan. As I crossed the second pass, the sun had sunk below the mountains behind me. The snow was coloured by the reflected evening light. Suddenly two snow leopards walked out from behind a buttress of rock not fifty yards ahead of me. They paused for a moment and looked at me, then ambled on across the snow, apparently quite unconcerned. It was the first time I had seen these beautiful creatures. In that wild and lovely setting it was a most moving experience.

I rode on until long after dark before reaching the little grazing-ground of Tarbashi, where there were two Kirghiz *akois* (dome-shaped, felt tents).[1] It was nearly eleven o'clock before all the caravan arrived. The Kirghiz gave us a warm welcome, provided us with food and milk and insisted that we spent the night in one of the *akois*. This was my first encounter with these mountain nomads, for although we had seen many of them south of Tashkurghan, we would not have been permitted to visit their *akois*, and they would have been much too frightened to have any intercourse with us. Each day that followed was as delightful as the last; each night we spent in an *akoi* with a Kirghiz family who gave us the impression that they were really pleased to see us and could not do enough for us. After crossing two more steep passes, we made our way down a valley, forty miles long, which took us gently down towards the plains. As we went, the mountains on either side became less steep and high. Near the foot of the valley we came to a series of villages, with square, flat-roofed mud-houses, terraced, irrigated fields and poplars, not unlike those in the upper Hunza Valley that we had left nearly three weeks before. We spent a night at one of these, in a house built around a square courtyard, with a high verandah, where we ate and slept, looking on to it. In the courtyard I was intrigued to see a large wooden cartwheel in the process of construction. Having travelled for so long among high mountains I had become so unaccustomed to the idea of wheeled traffic that I had quite forgotten that I would presently be coming to a country where it could be used.

The next day we emerged at last from the mountains. The valley widened out like an estuary of a river flowing into the sea. The river meandered over flat, stony ground and finally disappeared underground. We rode out into the desert.

[1] See page 117.

There was a thick dust haze over the country; the mountains behind became ghostly shapes and soon disappeared altogether. The march across this stretch of desert was an interlude between two worlds. The day before, as for many weeks past, we had been travelling through wild mountain country, with rushing torrents, huge rock precipices and lofty snow-peaks as the chief landmarks of our march. That evening we reached one of the great oases of the Tarim Basin: mile upon mile of flat, cultivated fields, divided by avenues of poplars, dusty paths, walled orchards, canals and sluggish streams flanked by willows; thickly populated, intimate country, yet strangely unlike anything I had ever seen. We reached Yangi Hisar as it was getting dark and put up in a caravan serai on the edge of the town.

The distance from Yangi Hisar to Kashgar is forty-three miles. I decided to ride ahead and cover it in a single day, while the rest of the caravan took the prescribed two. I started at dawn, and as my pony was tired after the journey I took it gently, so that it was dark before I reached Kashgar. In that time I was able to absorb much of the curious atmosphere of the country. There was still a dust haze, and though it was lighter than on the day before, I could not see the mountains which I knew to be away to my left. The sun, when it rose above the haze which had made it look like a squashed orange, was warm. Indeed, at noon and in the early afternoon it was almost oppressively hot, though it was already October, and the glare from the white, dusty road was trying. Most of the time I was in cultivated country; the fields were largely under plough, though in some, crops of maize and millet were still standing. From time to time I crossed a strip of desert, flat, stony ground, with tamarisk scrub, occasionally broken with high sand-dunes; but I was never out of sight of an oasis, marked on the horizon by a line of poplars. In a way it was dull, monotonous country, but it had a peculiar enchantment which I could not define, and which it never quite lost even when it became familiar.

Perhaps it owed some of its appeal to the fact that, though
it was a fertile land supporting a prosperous community,
nowhere was there any trace of Western culture to distort
its ancient, indigenous grace. But though, nowadays, that is
rare, it is not unique; and Southern Sinkiang has a quality
that is unique in my experience.

At the small town of Tazghun, half-way between Yangi
Hisar and Kashgar, it was market-day. As I approached it, I
became swept up in an ever-increasing throng of people
coming into the market from the surrounding villages. Most
of them were riding and carrying their goods on donkeys;
but there were also gaily-coloured "Peking carts" drawn by
ponies, ox-drawn wagons and strings of camels. It was a
cheerful procession. Everyone seemed to be talking and singing at the tops of their voices, oblivious of the choking dust.
They were surprisingly well-dressed in long, padded coats,
black leather riding-boots and embroidered skull-caps, black
and white or brightly coloured. Very few were ragged. Some
of the older men wore white turbans, denoting that they had
made the pilgrimage to Mecca. Many of the women, who
also wore padded coats and riding-boots, were veiled with
dark-blue material.

It was evening when I rode past Yangi Shahr, the New or
Chinese City of Kashgar. The light of the declining sun
seemed somehow to be absorbed into the great mud walls
that were all I could see of the town. I had still six miles to
go. Though I was tired and stiff, I hadn't the heart to urge
my pony into a trot. But it was pleasant riding slowly along
in the gathering dusk. The wide, green bed of the Kashgar
River was on my right, a line of loess cliffs beyond. It was
long after dark when I reached Kashgar and I had a good
deal of difficulty in finding the Consulate. It had been a long
final day to the journey from India, but it had given me a
fascinating introduction to the country where I was to spend
the next two years—a rather lonely and very exasperating
two years, unfortunately, but not without its compensations.

II

In broad outline the geography of Southern Sinkiang is simple. It consists of the Tarim Basin, a vast oval-shaped plain almost completely surrounded by high mountain ranges; the Kuen Lun on the south and south-east, the Pamirs on the south-west and west, merging into the Tien Shan which, running in an arc, nine hundred miles long, forms the northern rim of the Basin, and separates it from Northern Sinkiang. The rivers draining from these mountains, though many of them are fed from some of the largest snow-fields outside Polar regions, can do no more than irrigate a narrow fringe of country, resulting in a circular chain of oases nearly two thousand miles long, before they disappear into the arid interior of the Basin, which consists of the formidable Takla Makan Desert. When in 1937 we were battling with the flood waters of the Shaksgam, itself a mere tributary of the Yarkand River, it was difficult to believe that they would eventually be dissipated in this way. The majority of the streams disappear even before they reach the plains, though they add to the water-supply in the form of springs.

These glacier-fed rivers are the life-blood of Southern Sinkiang. For, though the precipitation of moisture in the high mountains is heavy, the rainfall in the plains is negligible (in Kashgar, for example, the average is about two and a half inches a year), and agriculture is entirely dependent on irrigation. The archæological researches of the late Sir Aurel Stein have shown that in ancient times great cities existed far out in what is now complete desert. From this it can be inferred that the extent of the oases was many times greater than it is to-day. Evidence that the desert is still encroaching is not difficult to find. Unless the present climatic trends are altered, it looks as though the plains of Southern Sinkiang will eventually become uninhabitable. But the process is far too slow to concern the present inhabitants of the country; and in any case our scientists and statesmen between them will probably have achieved the same result over the entire planet long before the desiccation of the Tarim Basin is complete. For the present population of the country the area under cultivation is adequate, and with improved methods of water conservation it could certainly be very greatly increased.

The people of the oases are mostly Turki; they are closely akin in race and language to the Ottoman Turkish. Their standard of living is comparatively high. With a plentiful supply of water from the mountains they make an easy livelihood from the fertile loess soil. Indeed, if one believes that progress is the key to human happiness, it may be that their life is a bit too easy. The most primitive methods of agriculture and irrigation suffice. Serious failure of crops because of drought or pestilence is almost unknown. The climate is not severe, and owing to the lack of rain the simplest mud-walled, flat-roofed houses are all that is required to withstand the weather. As a result, the people are placid and easy-going. Like most people who make an easy living from the land, they want more than anything else to be left alone. It is their unfortunate geographical position that has caused the centuries of strife which make up their turbulent history.

Kashgar, which lies at the western extremity of the great circle of oases surrounding the Takla Makan, is typical of the towns of Southern Sinkiang. The main part of the town is surrounded by a massive wall about fifty feet high, though it has overflowed the boundaries of the wall in a cluster of suburbs. The streets are narrow, though not unduly squalid. They are lined with the shops of metal-workers, potters, cloth-merchants, caterers, bakers and fruit-sellers. In the centre there is a large market-square and a mosque with a dome of blue tiles. An old Chinese temple stands high above the rest of the town, in curious contrast to the indigenous architecture.

I can best give an impression of the country around Kashgar by describing the scene which I saw for the first time the next morning from the terrace of the British Consulate-General; and, as I discovered later, the description can be applied, with minor modifications, to almost any oasis in Southern Sinkiang. From a high bluff shaded by tall chenar trees, I look across a stretch of fields to the river. The lanes between the fields are flanked by willows. A constant stream of people passes along them: bearded men in turbans and heavy, padded coats, young men in brightly coloured skull-caps, singing lustily, women in tent-like purdah garments. They are nearly all riding donkeys, for the Turkis never walk if they can possibly avoid it. Occasionally a camel cara-van appears, lumbering slowly along with a deep clang of bells. The camels are strung together in a long line and always led by a donkey. To the left, across a sunken road, there is another bluff slightly lower than ours, so that I can look down into a walled orchard of peach and apricot trees, and occasionally watch my neighbour, a rich man appar-ently, entertaining his friends with feast and music.

Across the river there is a line of buff-coloured loess cliffs upon which there are clusters of flat-roofed mud-houses, almost indistinguishable from the cliffs. Beyond, fields and orchards, willows and poplars, stretch away to the edge of the oasis. In the background the desert rises gently to a line of yellow hills, fluted and scored like the "Bad Lands" of Arizona. If the air is clear, I can see, through a gap in the hills, far away to the north, the western ranges of the Tien Shan. But on most days the view is restricted by a dust haze like a slightly foggy day at home, and I cannot see beyond the edge of the oasis, about five miles away.

This dust haze is a peculiar and rather unpleasant feature of Southern Sinkiang. I have never met anything quite like it elsewhere. I presume it is in part due to the unusual form and the geographical situation of the Tarim Basin, but I have seen no convincing explanation of its physical causes. Although there are wind-storms, they are not unusually frequent or persistent, and I have found that, in Kashgar at any rate, they usually precede a period of good visibility, while the dust haze is usually accompanied by a period of still weather. Again, in my experience, there is no time of year when clear periods are more likely to occur than at any other. On the average throughout the year there are perhaps two clear days in ten; but it would give a truer idea of the (very irregular) rhythm to say that three weeks of dust haze is followed by four or five days of clear air. Perhaps, for the foreign resident in Kashgar who cares for such things, the dust haze has one advantage: it certainly heightens the almost dramatic effect of the astonishing panorama that is revealed when it rolls away—the towering rock mountains far away to the north-east and north-west, the smaller desert hills that give distant perspective to the scene, the huge ice-peaks of the Pamirs that stand in a great, glistening arc to the south and south-west. Perhaps if one saw this every day, one would get used to it. I could never quite believe that I should.

In the winter the Kashgar scene is often drab and colour-less. There are no evergreens and scarcely any grass. Every-thing is brown and grey. The rice-fields are frozen. There are sheets of ice along either side of the wide, meandering river. Vapour rises from it into the frosty air. Flights of mallard, pochard and grey geese whirl back and forth in search of some unfrozen spring where they can feed. It seldom snows. About the middle of March a misty green appears on the willows. Then comes the fruit blossom in scattered drifts of pink and white. In April the lucerne appears in the fields and the young wheat, and, with the trees in new leaf, the whole countryside is swept by a flood of green. So sudden is the change that only two or three weeks seem to have separated deep, arid winter from the fullness of summer. The fig trees and grape vines are dug from the ground where they have been buried for protection from the frost. About the middle of May some of the fruit

begins to ripen. First apricots, then, in continuous series,
strawberries (only in the Consulate garden), mulberries,
cherries, nectarines, figs, peaches and grapes; pears and
apples, too, but they are indifferent. Most important of all
are the melons; for the melons of Southern Sinkiang are, I
think, the finest in the world. There are certainly none to
compare with them in the Middle East or in India; while
even the Hami *gwa*, famous throughout China, are not so
good as those of the Southern oases. I counted twenty-six
varieties. Some have a maximum girth of more than four
feet. They play a very important part in the lives of the
people. Melon stalls serve as wayside cafés where the thirsty
traveller can refresh himself by paying a few cents for a
juicy slice. In a market there seem to be almost as many
melon-sellers as the vendors of all other commodities put
together. If you call at a Turki house, the first thing you are
offered is a slice of melon. Traders carry them for many
days' journey up into the mountains to exchange with the
Kirghiz nomads for butter, meat and skins. A man can make
a very comfortable living by cultivating a few acres of
melons, though when the fruit is ripening (between July and
October, according to the variety), he and his family must
spend the nights in the fields to prevent theft. To get the
best prices, he must store the melons for sale in winter and
early spring, so that, except for about three months, they are
procurable the whole year round.

Yes, Kashgar was a pleasant place to live in; for anyone
with a taste for travel, with a sense of geography and with a
spark of curiosity about people and their ways there can be
few places in the world more satisfying. Though that great
scourge of modern civilization, the internal-combustion
engine, had, alas, made its appearance in Southern Sinkiang
a few years before, it was still a rarity, and still confined to
the immediate environs of Kashgar and to the two main
arterial highways, to Urumchi and to Khotan. All other
journeys had to be done with pony or camel caravan or on

foot, which are the only methods of travel that can provide a sense of intimacy with, and understanding of, the country. Despite the political influences at work, the people still pursued their ancient way of life; they and their country were as yet almost untouched by contact with the West. Although during my first two years there I was able to travel very little and to explore not at all; although the hostility, the boycotts and the general frustration were at times hard to bear, I was sorry to leave.

III

I travelled out by way of Soviet Turkestan and Persia. I was given an armed escort as far as the frontier at Irkestam. During the past few months the attitude of the local authorities towards our Consulate and towards Indian traders had undergone a remarkable change, and I was now treated with great friendliness and courtesy. By a curious chance the officer in charge of my escort was the one who had met me at Lup Gas the day after I had crossed the Mintaka Pass just over two years before. He appeared rather sheepish when I showed my recognition, but we soon laughed it off and became great friends. At Irkestam I was handed some Soviet currency which had been sent for me from Moscow. Beyond the frontier there was a first-class motor-road. I was travelling in a decrepit Russian lorry, driven by a delightful young Russian who talked hard all the time, heedless of the fact that I hardly understood a word he said. The scenery on this part of the journey was magnificent and I bitterly regretted that I could see it only from the cramped cab of the lorry. We were going down an immensely wide valley, to the south of which there was a vast panorama of ice-mountains of the Trans Alai Range. The road then crossed an 11,000-foot pass and descended steeply to the Feighana Plain. On the third day we reached Osh. Here I was placed under the charge of a charming girl who took me in a luxurious limousine to Andijan. We travelled at high speed along a broad tarmac road through fertile, cotton-growing country. At Andijan I boarded the night train for Tashkent. This swift, almost violent, transition from the slow tempo and medieval atmosphere of Sinkiang to the bustle and crowded turmoil of modern industrial life was fantastic. For a time I was in a daze, hardly able to take in half I saw.

Early the next morning I reached Tashkent. It was raining and the place looked dismal. I was met at the station by a seedy-looking individual who spoke to me in French. He told me that there would be a train on to Krasnavodsk soon, but no one could say quite when, and in the meantime a room had been reserved for me at an hotel, to which he escorted me. It was clearly the hotel-de-luxe of Tashkent; a relic of Tsarist times. It had the form of a good Continental hotel, with a wide staircase leading up from a spacious hall, but everything was in a state of advanced decay. My bedroom on the first floor was evidently the best in the place. It was a large, high-ceilinged room with french windows leading onto a balcony overlooking the street. The furnishings also dated from Tsarist times and obviously had not been renovated since. A vast gilt-framed mirror, with a great crack diagonally across it, occupied most of one wall, above a marble mantelpiece on which there were some coloured china ornaments. For the rest there was an iron bedstead, an upright, singularly uneasy chair, a hard settee and a dilapidated carpet. The following day I was moved to a mean room at the back, nearer to the evil-smelling lavatory. This was the worst thing about the hotel. None of the flushing systems in the half-dozen cubicles worked, nor had they done so, apparently, for some years. Nor was there anyone whose job it was to make good this deficiency by cleaning them out. The resulting filth and stench were indescribable.

I stayed in Tashkent for four days. Hitherto I had been quite impressed with my first brief glimpse of Soviet Turkestan. Osh had had an appearance of well-ordered prosperity. The country between there and Andijan looked well organized and well cultivated. I was very disappointed in Tashkent. In Kashgar, one of the most common Soviet propaganda posters was a somewhat impressionistic representation of Tashkent; rather like a glorified edition of those fantastically palatial factories pictured in the advertisements of biscuit manufacturers. It showed spacious boulevards, flanked by wide stretches of parkland, leading up to superb modern buildings. The streets certainly were wide; there were tramways and there was a not-unpleasant little park where one could sit in the sun and gaze at large busts of Lenin and Stalin. But the place was terribly drab; there was nowhere the charm of an old Asiatic town, nor anything of the efficient comfort of a modern city. There was nothing to relieve the monotony of the square concrete and plaster buildings, which were all shabby, while many revealed their active decomposition by great cracks in the walls.

Beyond the ordinary curiosity aroused by a new country, and one normally so inaccessible to a Western traveller, I found little to interest me in Tashkent and nothing to admire. But two things struck me most forcibly. One was the very high proportion of the million or so inhabitants who seemed to be European Russians. Certainly it was not always possible in their uniform European clothing to tell whether the people I saw were European or Asiatic, but even allowing for that, the number of the former was most striking. The other was the quite remarkable poverty of the food. I had only that provided by my hotel to go on, but judging by the crowds of non-residents that assembled in the restaurant at mealtimes, it can hardly have been considered much below the average. The only dish I ever succeeded in obtaining in the restaurant was a thin vegetable—and occasionally meat—stew and bread. The bread was very dark brown and tasted of coarse brown cardboard, which seemed to stick in one's throat. Sometimes the kind chambermaid in charge of my room brought me a couple of eggs, but I gathered these

were not normally provided. Russia had been at war for little
more than a year.

Each evening my French-speaking friend came to pay me
a brief visit to tell me that the time of my train had not yet
been announced. At length, one morning he came with the
news that the train was approaching and would leave at
noon. He took me to the station in a car. On the way he
pressed into my hand a parcel, furtively, as though it were
opium; it contained two white-bread rolls. The train pulled
out at about half-past two. It had come from Moscow, which
it had left a week before, and was crowded with troops
bound for Krasnavodsk, on the Caspian Sea, and thence, I
gathered, for the Caucasus front. I was provided with a
fairly comfortable upper berth in one of the officers' car-
riages. The troops travelled on wooden seats in squalid,
badly sprung trucks and they bore the marks of their week's
journey.

The railway, which had been built in Tsarist times, was
still a single-tracked affair, with sidings at regular intervals
to allow the trains to pass each other. Troop trains were
evidently of low priority, for ours never seemed to have the
right-of-way and always drew into the siding to wait for
oncoming trains to pass. The reason for this was that the
supply route up the Volga having been cut by the German
advance to Stalingrad, the urgently needed oil supplies were
being sent by this roundabout route to the northern fronts.
We passed about a dozen oil-trains a day. Our progress was
thus exceedingly slow, and it took three days to cover the
850 miles from Tashkent to Ashkabad, my destination; an
average of about twelve miles an hour. The way passed by
Samarkand and Bukhara, but from the train I saw nothing
of these romantic-sounding places, for they both lay some
miles from the railway. The journey, from the scenic
point of view, was intensely dull. Almost the whole
way there was nothing to be seen but stony desert, featureless and dead flat; no living creature was to be seen and

scarcely any human habitation, save an occasional mud-village clustered round a station. I was even denied the mild excitement of seeing the Oxus, for we crossed it at night. The frequent halts, however, had one advantage; one could avoid using the lavatory, which, after a momentary inspection, I did; it was in the same repulsive condition as that in my Tashkent hotel. There was a restaurant car on the forward part of the train, where twice a day a watery vegetable stew and "cardboard" bread was served. On the third day there was a sudden violent rush towards the restaurant car. My compartment mates generously explained the cause of the excitement, thus enabling me to secure a place in the forefront of the rush and a plate of meat stew.

The monotony of the journey was relieved by my travelling companions, who were most friendly and hospitable, as Russians always are when they are not being official. At first their interest in me appeared mainly due to the fact that I was expected to know the exact date of the opening of the Second Front. But when it became evident that I was not to be induced to disclose military secrets, and under the mellowing effect of vodka, supplies of which were replenished at each halt, intercourse became more convivial, though no more intelligible, and the time passed pleasantly enough in song and simple card-games. A young officer in the next compartment spoke excellent English. He found me out on the morning after we left Tashkent and thereafter took me under his benevolent protection. He was a tremendous talker and I was surprised by the openness with which he discussed political problems. By the second day he had become irresistibly attracted by my Rolex wrist-watch. He kept bringing the conversation round to the subject of watches. Watches, he said, were impossible to obtain in Russia. How could one fight a war without a watch? He had heard that they were plentiful in India where I was going. I resolutely ignored the hints. It was not that I minded his having my watch, but I hate being without one on a journey,

and I still had a long way to go. At length he was forced
into the open and made me an offer for it of two thousand
roubles (about £44 at the official rate of exchange). The
money would have been quite useless to me, for there was
little I could buy with it, and I could not take it out of the
country nor change it into foreign currency. I protested that
it was a very old watch and that I did not expect it to go for
much longer. However, nothing but a rude refusal would
have deflected him from his purpose, and at last I yielded,
and exchanged my beloved watch for a couple of bottles of
vodka, in which we drank to the eternal friendship between
our two countries.

At Ashkabad I bade farewell to my kind companions, a
particularly fond one to my English-speaking friend. I was not
met, and had to make my way to the hotel by myself, lugging
a hugely expanded suitcase. The distance seemed about two
miles, but as I had great difficulty in finding the place, it
may, in fact, have been less. I made several abortive enquiries (of the "stranger-here-myself" type), but at length
happened upon an English-speaking Pole who took me
along with marked enthusiasm. Thereafter he became a persistent, though somewhat secretive, visitor. After a bit I
began to suspect that some motive other than the charm of
my company lay behind this display of *bonhomie*. Towards
the end of my stay, when we were alone together behind
carefully closed doors, he unburdened his long and heart-
breaking story. He was by trade a film-producer who had
been uprooted from his home in Poland at the beginning of
the war, suffered terrible privations with his wife and small
children and had somehow (I forget exactly how) landed
up, still with his family, in this remote spot, where naturally
he did not find much scope for his vocation. He sought my
help to get him out. Of course, there was nothing I could do
for him beyond promising to visit his brother who was living
in Kensington and pass on the news of his whereabouts and
the story of his odyssey. This I did. Another frequent, and

at first somewhat surprising visitor, was my English-speaking officer friend from the train. He turned up the morning after I had arrived, when I was thinking of him as tossing on the Caspian Sea. He explained casually that he was an engineer and had something to do with the railway. I suppose he had just forgotten to tell me that he too was getting off at Ashkabad; or perhaps it had had something to do with the watch transaction. However, I was delighted to see him and my time again passed pleasantly enough, drinking vodka and talking.

Ashkabad I found to be built on much the same lines as Tashkent, but it was a comparatively small place without the noise, bustle and crowds, so that on the whole it was no more drab and depressing than, say, Toulouse after the German occupation. Moreover, close at hand were the mountains of the Persian frontier, whose shapes and colours, though not especially exciting in themselves, provided a great relief from the intolerable flatness of the country over which I had lately been travelling. Typical, I imagine, of most of the towns of Soviet Turkestan, the centre of Ashkabad was marked by a vast parade—or meeting—ground presided over by an elegant concrete rostrum or saluting-base. Apparently the absence or obstruction of public conveniences presented as big a problem to the local populace as they had to me, for on closer inspection I found that not only the ground immediately surrounding it but the spacious steps and platform of the rostrum itself were covered deeply with deposits of evil-smelling filth.

I stayed two nights in Ashkabad, and then late on the third I was given a place on one of a convoy of lorries, and was taken to the Russian frontier post about ten miles away. Here my baggage was given a cursory examination, I surrendered the remainder of my roubles, and waited for dawn, when I got a lift on another lorry to a tiny village a few miles on the Persian side of the frontier. From here to Meshed I had to hitch-hike. There should have been no lack of traffic on this part of the road, as it was one of the lesser arteries in the already active "Supplies to Russia" system. My main problem was money; not a problem exactly, for I had none. I had brought some food with me from Kashgar, but for transport I had to rely upon the goodwill of the Persian lorry-drivers. After waiting a day in the village, I got a lift down to Kuchan, and after thirty-six hours there, another to Meshed.

At Meshed I had two days of ease and luxury at the British Consulate-General. The Consul-General, Mr. C. P. (now Sir Clarmont) Skrine, had been one of my predecessors in Kashgar. He himself was unfortunately away in India at the time, but Mrs. Skrine welcomed me with very great kindness. She had been with her husband in Kashgar in the palmy days of the early 'twenties and had loved every moment of it; so that I was able to indulge in that very rare luxury for a returning traveller—unlimited talk with a sympathetic audience about the subject which is nearest his heart. Under her expert guidance, too, I saw a lot of Meshed, including a private view of the famous Blue Mosque.

The remainder of my way to India consisted of three days by lorry to Zahidan, and thirty-six hours in the weekly train from Zahidan to Quetta. In many ways it had been an interesting journey from Kashgar, and I would not have missed it. But had it been my only experience of travel across the great spaces of Central Asia, I would have been sadly disillusioned. Fortunately, I had done enough to realize that even to-day most travel in Central Asia must be done by less banal methods.

CHAPTER III

BOSTAN TEREK—A GLISSADE

HERE are those, I believe, who imagine that the number of unexplored and unclimbed mountains is fast running out; that given reasonably peaceful conditions, quicker and cheaper transport, in a generation or so, half a century at most, all the peaks of the world will have been scaled, and that, even in the more remote ranges, mountaineers wishing to tread new ground will have to "invent" new ways of approach. That must indeed be a gloomy prospect. But I defy even the most pessimistic mountaineer to travel far in the highlands of Central Asia and still to hold that view. He may come to wonder, as I have often wondered, whether in a century and a half of mountaineering, one-tenth of the summits of the world have as yet been reached.

For the first thirty years of this century, the huge panorama of ice-mountains seen from Ranikhet contained only one peak (Trisul) that had been climbed. Those mountains are the most easily accessible in the Himalaya. Imagine, if you can, several hundred such ranges. One of them I can see from the roof of my house in Kashgar. From here on a clear day I can count a score of peaks without name, without position on any map, unmeasured. Not amorphous desert hills that no one would want to climb anyway; not the 25,000-foot giants that would demand the tiresome organization of "high camps" and "assault parties"; not "aiguilles," "nordends" or subsidiary summits (I could use the word hundreds if I included those). They are peaks of Alpine stature and form, each rising from its own system of glacier valleys and supported by its own complex of granite face and ice-ridge. Any one of them could be climbed by a competent

35

party, after due reconnaissance and failure, from a camp barely above the pine forest. Many of them would offer problems as attractive as any in the Alps. Yet I doubt whether by the end of the twentieth century much more will be known about these peaks, in climbing terms, than is known to-day. Not because of "iron curtains"; not because they lie far from the offices and homes of those interested in these matters; but simply because of the vastness of the field for new mountaineering adventure of which they form so small a part.

It may well be objected that the existence of such a field is scant consolation to those whose brief holidays confine them to overcrowded Alpine peaks. But, even so, it is well for them to contemplate this wider background, to realize that the future of mountaineering does not consist only in the unending development of gymnastic technique, and that though the advance of modern means of transport may shrink the world to lamentably small proportions, it should also continue, for a very long time to come, to open an ever-expanding field of mountaineering enterprise. Let us not waste our sympathy on posterity; there will be enough for them as there is for us.

On even the most familiar journeys in this part of the world, unexplored ranges are such a commonplace, so much the order of the marching day, that to cross a side-stream whose source is known usually calls for excited comment; a peak distinguished with a name stands like a lighthouse in a limitless sea. This is enchanting, no doubt, but over-familiarity with these conditions has, I find, one unfortunate and rather disconcerting result. I appear to have lost a good deal of my interest in climbing mountains. Not entirely; but much of the rapturous enthusiasm seems to have gone. I recall, for example, my intense eagerness to make the second ascent of Mount Kenya, which for some months was a ruling passion of my life, and with some sadness contrast it with the nonchalance with which I gaze at a view of half a dozen peaks, greater in height, equally beautiful in form. I am not alone in this. I have often remarked, for example, how little members of the Mount Everest expeditions used to avail themselves of the opportunity, for many of them unique, of climbing virgin peaks around the Base Camp or in Sikkim. The excuse was rarely valid that the exhaustion of high climbing or lack of time prevented them. Everest has all too seldom allowed us to exhaust ourselves on her higher reaches; few, surely, have calculated their time with such precision as to have to deny themselves an extra week, even if as much were needed.

How, then, are we to explain this away? Is it an ugly reflection upon the purity of our motive? Is the fame of a mountain a necessary part of the stimulus that makes us wish to climb it? Must we be able to point out our conquest to an appreciative audience and say "I climbed that"? Do we wonder, even subconsciously, what is the use of climbing one of a range of a thousand mountains that nobody has even heard of? I have tried to account for this disturbing tendency in myself by the reflection that mountain-climbing has its roots in a desire to explore; that given the genuine article, the substitute loses much of its allure. There is a good deal of truth in this, but the explanation is far from being entirely satisfactory. It cannot be claimed that much exploration was done on the later Everest expeditions. It does not account for the fact that in my present mood I would undoubtedly be more stirred by a view of the Peuterey Ridge than by a ridge of twice the size on an unknown mountain. Nor does it explain my acute feelings of envy when I read a friend's account of his ascent of the Gugi Route or of the Vieraselgrat. Such things should be paltry beside my own opportunities, if not my exploits. But they often seem a great deal more desirable. I have wondered if this is not due to my advancing years; whether I am not becoming an armchair mountaineer, ready to envy but not to act. But I think I can honestly (if eagerly) reject this explanation. For I am satisfied that were I to visit the Alps again, my enthusiasm for climbing peaks would be little or no less than it was twenty years ago. Unfortunately, in that period I have only had one brief opportunity of putting the speculation to the test. I found, in those two days, infinite satisfaction in being once more in country, every inch of which was accurately mapped, the smallest buttress named. I set out to climb a third-rate mountain as eagerly as though it had been my first expedition with rope and axe.

It seems, then, that we must look for some deeper reason for the failure of these unknown mountains to attract us to their remote and lonely summits; for we must at all costs avoid the indictment of a competitive spirit. An analogy might perhaps be allowed in the case of rock-climbing. Does the Lakeland expert gaze with longing at the great rock walls of the Lauterbrunnen Valley as he passes them in the train? Would he be consumed by an irresistible desire to force his way up one of an infinite number of possible routes on a twenty-mile-long precipice flanking the path up the Hunza Valley? Would he not be overcome by a feeling of cold futility if he tried? Like most analogies it exaggerates the case; and, of course, it will be argued that while there are great peaks to be climbed, one does not bother with minor buttresses, that, in fact, as mountain-climbing is a substitute for mountain exploration, so cliff-climbing is a substitute for mountain-climbing. This, too, may be allowed, but again I find it an unsatisfactory explanation. There *is* some quality about a buttress on Scafell that urges us to climb it, which is lacking in a cliff that is less well-known by reason of the very profusion of precipices in which it is set. So, I find, it is with mountains themselves. Some kind of intimacy, either personal or historical, seems to be necessary, without which we are oppressed by an overwhelming sense of loneliness and awed by the insignificance of our achievement.

The best way to cure a mountaineer of such unhealthy introspection is to deny him access to the mountains. Until my first tour in Kashgar, I had never been in the position of being able to gaze month after month at mountains with little or no prospect of reaching them. It was not an unmitigated torment. There was so much joy and solace in just looking at them in their never-ending variety of cloud and colour setting, that I certainly would not have wished them away. The memory that there had been periods in my life when I was completely satisfied by physical contact with great peaks was an enormous help in curbing regret and in preventing it from spoiling the contemplation of that remarkable view.

Even so, there were times when the craving to reach the mountains was almost intolerable. For in those days in Kashgar I was living in a police state. Moreover, I and my fellow-nationals were unlucky enough to be fulfilling that important political rôle performed by the Jews under Hitler and by the bourgeoisie during the French Revolution. A scapegoat is apparently necessary to a dictatorship, at least in its earlier years. Later, of course, the species is liable to become extinct through failure of the authorities to observe even the most elementary rules of game preservation, and the ruling clique must seek or invent some external object for its righteous abuse. The excellent band of Swedish missionaries who had done such fine work here for the best part of half a century and had won the universal respect and liking of the local population, being more vulnerable to attack, had succumbed a couple of years before. The Indian traders clung to life with unreasonable tenacity, and we stayed to support them. Between us we served their purpose. Any official or private individual whom the authorities found it convenient to remove was at once found to have been friendly with, or spying for, the British Consulate-General. I discovered later that our sinister influence had spread far and wide: in distant cities that no Indian trader or member of our staff had

visited for a quarter of a century; among Kirghiz tribesmen
in remote mountain valleys, who had never set eyes upon our
humble establishment. The resulting boycott was tiresome,
but I found it easy to bear compared to the confinement to a
ten-mile radius in the midst of this country of such bound-
less opportunity.

At length, after nearly a year, I could stand it no longer,
and I decided to slink away in secret to the nearest mountains. At the time I attributed the success of my plan to my
cleverness in its execution. I later discovered that, a thousand
miles away in the Provincial capital, forces were at work
which were to result in a complete political *volte-face,* and
which ended for a time that ugly spell of totalitarian rule.
But for this, I am more than doubtful whether I would have
achieved my innocent design. However that may be, I left
Kashgar before dawn one morning in September in a covered
country cart, together with Lhakpa Tenzing and a Hunza
servant, and after two long days' travel reached the Kirghiz
settlement of Bostan Terek, sixty miles to the west.

The first day's march was through the south-westward
extension of the Kashgar oasis, along dusty country roads,
flanked by willows, irrigation channels and fields, to Opal.
This I thought was the danger-point, and though we passed
through the bazaar in the dusk, I was fully expecting to be
challenged and asked for our papers. However, we got
through without a hitch, spent the night at the edge of the
oasis, and were off again by dawn the next morning. Once
out in the desert beyond Opal I breathed a sigh of relief, for
I then felt fairly safe from pursuit. It was a long, hot, waterless march, utterly monotonous, over gently rising ground,
rocky and scored by innumerable dry water-courses. But the
mountains were in view, and though we seemed to be moving infinitely slowly, they were gradually getting nearer.
Though we could see Bostan Terek the whole time, it was
not easy to find the track, and once off it the going was
terribly rough for our clumsy cart. We were still five or six

miles from our destination when night fell. Luckily we found a spring of water and, as there was plenty of dry tamarisk wood, we made a pleasant camp. We reached Bostan Terek early on the third morning.

We were sure of a friendly reception, for the Swedish missionaries had made a summer resort in the valley, to which they had come in relays each year. I knew that they had been very well liked, and that I would benefit from a reflection of that popularity; but, even so, I was not prepared for the warmth of the welcome we received. Every family seemed to vie with each other to entertain us. If their hospitality had not been so charmingly simple and genuine, it might have been embarrassing. They seemed to think that our arrival heralded a return to the good old days. We spent the remainder of the morning drinking milk in various *akois* and talking to our hosts. It was wonderful to be away from the atmosphere of fear and suspicion, that in those days ruled in the large oases. I spent the afternoon shooting chikor (hill partridge) of which there were thousands in the foot-hills nearby. I shot some dozens without any difficulty and distributed them to our hosts.

Bostan Terek is one of the eastern valleys of the Kashgar Range, a northerly continuation of the Pamirs. The river flowing down it from the glaciers at its head disappears when it leaves the foot-hills, under the thirty-mile-wide band of coarse alluvial deposits which we had just crossed. The water emerges again in springs, helps to irrigate the Opal oasis and eventually flows into the Yarkand River. At the foot of the valley there is enough water for the cultivation of quite a wide area of fields, where the Kirghiz grow wheat and barley. Like most of the Kirghiz of these parts they are semi-nomadic, grazing their flocks on the high pastures during the summer and living at the foot of the valley in winter. I have often wondered why these semi-nomads, who always inhabit the same valley, continue to live in *akois*, moving them from the arable land to the various levels of pasture and back

again according to the season. It would be easy enough for
them to build stone and timber houses at each place, which
would far outlast their frail tents, and save the continual
transport back and forth. They have told me that they dislike houses as they are difficult to keep clean and are apt to
become vermin-ridden.

The following day Lhakpa and I set off up the valley,
together with two Kirghiz and a couple of yaks we had hired
to carry our baggage. After we had passed through the cultivated area, we climbed up onto the wide, grassy ridge of
an ancient moraine. To the left, across a gorge cut by the
river, the southern flank of the valley was covered with fir
forest for several miles, until it merged into sheer granite
cliffs. Beyond, the valley floor climbed in a series of wide,
grassy terraces into the heart of the ice-mountains. We
camped in a pleasant little hollow by a spring at a height of
about thirteen thousand feet. From there, during the following week, Lhakpa and I did a series of climbs of varying
difficulty. I had brought my dog, Khombu, with me. We
had, of course, to leave him tied up when we set off each
morning, telling the Kirghiz to let him free when we had
been gone an hour. Each evening as we came off the glaciers
we would start shouting and he would come up to meet us.

It was a perfect place for a climbing holiday. A short way
above our camp the valley opened out into a wide circle of
granite peaks between 17,000 feet and 18,500 feet high.
Several glaciers draining from these met in the centre and
flowed a short way down the main valley. The highest peak
was a lovely twin-headed one which formed a prominent
landmark in the view from Kashgar. I had hoped to attempt
it after we had got into some sort of training on the
smaller mountains. It looked very difficult indeed. It was
built of a remarkable complexity of sharp granite ridges
divided by steep ice-couloirs and hanging glaciers. Each day
we studied it from a new angle, hoping to find some way
through its formidable defences. But each aspect looked

more forbidding than the last, and at length I decided reluctantly to abandon any idea of attempting it. We had neither the time nor the facilities for exploring the western aspect of the mountain, and the standard of climbing involved in an attempt on any route on the eastern side was obviously higher than anything we were likely to reach on this visit.

The second-highest peak in the group was also a very fine one, which resembled the Dent Blanche seen from the upper Zinal valley. The side of it facing the cirque was a granite precipice standing some four thousand feet sheer above the glacier. But just beyond a high col on the main watershed I had caught a profile glimpse of a face in its upper part which seemed to offer a possible route. The lower part was hidden behind the col. So on the sixth day, after we had done several climbs, we set out to reconnoitre.

The way to the col led through a glacier bay shut in by the great rock walls of the highest and the second-highest peaks, and thence up a long snow-couloir. As we were making our way up the glacier bay there was an eclipse of the sun. At this point it was not a total eclipse (the edge of the belt of totality was about a hundred miles to the north), but it was sufficiently complete to produce a weird effect of deep twilight. We reached the col before noon. From it we saw the whole of the face of our mountain. The lower part was an easy snow-slope which we could reach without any difficulty by climbing a couple of hundred feet down beyond the col. The upper part consisted of a band of broken rocks split by a very steep snow- or ice-couloir. Above the rocks an ice-dome formed the summit of the mountain. To reach it from our camp would involve a climb of more than five thousand feet. But the difficult section was comparatively small. Much depended upon the quality of the snow on the lower part of the face.

We started the next morning just before dawn. Like each of its predecessors, it was a lovely day. Although as soon as the sun rose we were in its light, it was very cold and the snow remained frozen hard all the way up to the col. We made much better time than on the previous day. But on the face of the mountain beyond the col the snow deteriorated extraordinarily quickly, and before we had gone a thousand feet up it we were sinking in well above our knees. This was an unpleasant surprise, for after at least a week of fine weather, and probably much longer, I could see no reason for such a depth of soft snow. The slow, upward struggle consumed hours of time, with almost imperceptible results.

As we approached the rocks, the slope became steeper and the snow firmer. We had intended to climb the couloir which split the rock face, but as we came nearer to it we saw that it was composed of hard, blue ice. It was tremendously steep and it would have taken us at least six hours to cut steps to the top of it. As it was already nearly one o'clock by the time we reached the foot of the rocks, this was clearly out of the question. The rocks themselves did not look too difficult. We chose a line and started to climb them. Here we met with our third disappointment. The rocks were completely rotten, coated with ice and a great deal steeper than they had appeared from below. It was the kind of ground, common on broken, ice-covered rocks, where it appears that if one can only overcome the next ten feet it will be much easier and where this appearance always turns out to be wrong. We climbed some way up a nasty little gully and were defeated by a slippery scoop, only ten feet high, at its top. With great difficulty we traversed across to a rib to the left. Here we found that the rock was firmer and comparatively free from ice. I decided that we should give the rib a trial and if we failed to climb it we should abandon the attempt.

After a couple of pitches the rib steepened a lot and the climbing became very difficult. But by then we were only a hundred feet below the base of the ice-dome forming the summit. I led off in a determined attempt to reach it, supposing that the difficulties would then be over. I had already conceived the idea of glissading down the ice-couloir as an alternative to climbing down the rocks. Though it was steep and narrow and composed entirely of ice, there was a perfect run out at the bottom and providing we kept our feet we could not come to any harm. The idea appealed to me so much that I pressed my efforts on the upper part of the rib a good deal farther than I ought to have done. I climbed very slowly. It was difficult all the way and there was absolutely no stance, let alone a belay to which I could bring Lhakpa. I had almost reached the ice when the rope came taut behind me. I could not possibly have held Lhakpa, who in any case said, very wisely, that in the circumstances he would rather not follow. I had either to retreat or unrope and go on to the top, perform my wild glissade and then return to fetch Lhakpa, who fortunately was in a comfortable position. The prospect of climbing down the way I had come was so abhorrent that I decided on the latter course.

I unroped and threw down the end, thus effectively burning my boats. I then climbed the remaining few feet to the top of the rocks. Here to my dismay I found that my difficulties were by no means over. The base of the ice-dome was flush with the top of the rocks and there was no ledge between the two. Moreover, for the first four feet the ice was vertical, before it gradually began to slope back. At the top of the rib there was one foot-hold, flat but only large enough to take the sole of one boot. With infinite caution, by a sort of "mantelpiece" movement, I managed, after two attempts, to stand with my left foot on this. It was a horrible position, for at first there was nothing to hold on to, and the bulge of the ice seemed to be pushing me outwards off my balance. I remember wondering how many times I would bounce if I fell, before reaching the snow-slope below. I swung my axe above my head and dug the pick into the ice. That helped matters, but it was not a permanent relief and I had to face the unpleasant task of cutting a step in the ice. Fortunately, immediately to my right, the face of the ice, though still vertical, receded in conformity with the contour of the rock, which allowed me to swing my axe much more freely than would otherwise have been the case. First I cut a hand-hold well above the four-foot vertical section, and then, holding on to this with my gloved left hand, began work on the step. It was very laborious; for the step had to be large, as it would be awkward to step into it, and also knee-room had to be fashioned above. After every dozen or so strokes I had to rest my right arm. Also my left foot was getting very tired and I had often to relieve the pressure on it by anchoring my axe in the ice-slope above and leaning on it and the hand-hold. I must have worked on that step for well over half an hour before I was satisfied with it. I had cut it too high for convenience and had a struggle to get on to it. But once there, the relief was intense. The weight at last off my left foot, I could lean forward over the ice-bulge. The second and third steps were easy to make, and after that I was standing squarely on the ice-slope above. Soon, as the angle eased off, there was a covering of firm snow on the ice, and presently I could stop cutting and kick steps instead. I almost ran up the last slope, and five minutes later I reached the top of the mountain.

It was a quarter-past four. The air was calm, and the sun was still quite warm. I was still feeling the blissful relief of no longer being plastered against the ice-bulge. To this was now added the thrill of reaching the summit, of which I had several times during the day almost abandoned hope, and which latterly had become merely a way of escape. For a moment I almost forgot the unpleasant prospect of the glissade to which I was now committed. I would like to have sat for an hour studying the view. But I could not afford more than ten minutes; as it was, there was no chance of getting back to camp before dark. To the south, the peaks of the Kungur and Chakragil massifs were clear. But the best part of the view was to the north where stood the highest mountain of the Bostan Terek group. I was only a little lower than its twin summits, and its clean-cut, sweeping ridges stood out, magnificently defined in the slanting sunlight. I had no camera with me. In those days in Sinkiang cameras were strictly forbidden and it would have been asking for trouble to carry one.

It was nearly half-past four by the time I started the descent. I walked a little way along the wide summit ridge, and then started diagonally down to the right until I was immediately above the ice-couloir. A shout came from below and, looking down, I saw that Lhakpa had already climbed down to the snow-slope below the rocks. I cut a few steps down until I could get a clear view of the whole length of the couloir. It was dead straight, but very narrow in its middle section. It was essential that I should start exactly above this narrow part, for, once started, I could not possibly control the direction of my glissade. I cut a large platform from which to start, and stood for a few minutes contemplating the prospect with a sinking heart. It was much more frightening than I had expected. The ice was tremendously steep; Lhakpa and the blessed snow-slope looked miles away down; though the length of the couloir was not more than a few hundred feet; the two crags projecting from its sides half-way down allowed distressingly little room for error. However, there was nothing for it but to take the plunge, and the sooner I did so, the sooner I would get it over. It was at least, very simple; all I had to do was to keep my head, keep my legs and my body absolutely rigid, and hang on to my ice-axe for all I was worth. I leant hard back with my right hand almost on the ferrule of the axe (even so I seemed to be standing almost upright) and let my feet slip out of the step. The next moment I seemed to be falling through space with hardly any contact on the ice. The rushing wind caught my breath, but at the same time I felt as if I were shouting at the top of my voice. It seemed endless; but I was dimly aware of the rock promontories rushing up

towards me, and then past me, one on either side. I had no
time to realize that my aim through the narrow section had
been true before a wave of snow rushed up and blinded me.
Then after a while I felt my pace slacken. I dug my heels in,
came to a halt and sank down on the snow, completely
winded.

For the second time in about an hour I experienced a
glorious sense of relief. The summit had been reached and
the somewhat unorthodox descent of the only difficult part
achieved. Nothing remained but a long but easy downward
journey in the soft evening light. While I lay on the snow-
slope recovering my breath, Lhakpa came across to join me.
My hat had disappeared. I made no attempt to look for
it. We roped up and plunged on down the slope. The slight
rise from the foot of the face to the col demanded unwelcome
effort, but the snow in the couloir beyond was sufficiently
firm for a gentle glissade. Darkness fell as we were making
our way over the rough, moraine-covered lower glacier. But
soon we had the camp-fire to guide us. Khombu came up to
meet us in answer to our shouts. The Kirghiz, bless them,
had a pot of boiling water ready for us, and tea was soon
made.

The next day we went down and camped by the river
below the fir forest on the southern side of the valley. There,
in delightful contrast to the peaks and glaciers, we spent our
last three days, hunting ram chikor.

These remarkable birds are widely distributed in the high
mountains of Central Asia. I have found them in the Mount
Everest region, all over the Karakorams, in the Pamirs and
in the Tien Shan, at altitudes varying from 9,000 feet to
17,000 feet. Their taste in local environment seems to be
equally catholic. In early spring I have found them high up
on the tops of mountains covered by a deep mantle of snow,
with no bare ground to be seen for miles around; in the
summer I have found them living in pine forest; I have met

CHAKRAGIL FROM TASHMALIK

KIRGHIZ

TURKI

with them many miles up great glaciers and amongst barren mountains where water is very hard to find. They are large grey birds, sometimes as big as a small turkey. Their flesh is delicious. Hunting them with a shot-gun is, I find, even better sport than hunting ibex or *ovis poli*.

At dawn their echoing call, a long ascending note, can be heard high up on the mountain-side. It is the most thrilling sound I know; it seems somehow to express perfectly the wild grandeur of the country in which they live. Even with the call as a guide, it is generally difficult to locate them from a distance; and the first essential in hunting them is to spot them before they are aware of your presence. Except in the mating season, they keep together in flocks of twenty, thirty, or even more. They are difficult to stalk because one of their number usually sits perched on a rock commanding the surrounding mountain-side while the others are feeding, ready to give warning of an approaching enemy. When they are startled into flight or wish to fly to another grazing-ground, they launch themselves into a steep downward glide, thus gaining tremendous speed, which carries them in a sort of pendulum swing across the valley without any apparent wing movement. The beginning of the flight is nearly always accompanied by a shrill, gobbling cry.

It is no use attempting to shoot them on the wing, for they are always in steep country, high above the valley floor, and even if you were lucky enough to hit one, the speed of its flight would carry the dead bird such a distance that it would be almost impossible to find. The problem, then, with a shot-gun, is to get within thirty yards of them before they take off. It would be easier, of course, to shoot them with a rifle, but that is liable to ruin most of the flesh. If they are approached from above, they invariably take off as soon as they are disturbed and it is almost impossible to get a shot at them. But if they see you coming from below, they start running up-hill and usually do not launch into flight until within range. I have found that, when I am fresh and in good training, I can, by going all out, run up-hill a little faster than they can. But at that speed, after a few hundred feet, I can no longer gain on them. My stalks were rarely so successful that I could get within range of them unobserved, and they usually ended with a long up-hill chase which left me so winded that I often failed to hit the birds even if I got near enough. The best that I generally hoped for was to get so close before exposing myself that an upward dash of only two or three hundred feet would put me within range.

But sometimes the chase would go on for thousands of feet. For even when, as often happened, the birds spotted me a long way below and started their upward trek, all was not lost. If I could contrive to disappear again from their view they would loiter, thus enabling me to gain on them without exhausting myself by climbing too fast. The difficulty, then, was to keep on their track and still remain hidden. Lhakpa would co-operate from far below indicating their whereabouts with wild and usually unintelligible gesticulations.

In the matter of rock-climbing the ram chikor could always beat me, for they could flutter from ledge to ledge far faster than I could climb. So when they got on to cliffs I would have to try to outflank them, which often led to some very interesting mountaineering problems.

In all the scores of ram chikor stalks I have done, I doubt if more than one in ten has been successful. But whatever the result, they have always provided wonderful sport. On this occasion I was either exceptionally fit or, more likely, the birds were unusually fat and lazy after a whole summer of good eating, for in the three days I succeeded in shooting no fewer than six.

CHAPTER IV

POLITICAL BACKGROUND

BEFORE considering recent events in Sinkiang it is as
well to reflect upon its history during the present century. From this the salient fact emerges that from the
foundation of the Chinese Republic until 1942 there was
virtually no Central Government control over the Province.
In the general confusion that followed the revolution in
China in 1911 Yang Tseng-hsin came over from Kansu
where he had held the post of Governor, and took complete
charge of the Province. For the next seventeen years he ruled
with absolute authority, taking no orders from the Central
Government and submitting to no foreign influence. The
weakness of the Central Government and events in Russia
made it easy for him to retain his independence. What was
remarkable was the way in which he established and held
firm control throughout the Province. He rarely left his
capital in Urumchi and, so far as I know, never visited the
great southern oases. Yet he managed largely to prevent the
establishment of local tyranny, to restrain corruption within
reasonable limits and to avoid serious unrest thoughout the
whole vast area, where modern means of transport and communication were still quite unknown. It was an era of peace
and prosperity which many of the older inhabitants think of
as a golden age. For Indian traders this was certainly so.

How long Yang could have maintained this admirable state
of affairs in the face of increasing external pressure is a
matter for speculation, for in 1928 he was murdered. By
whose agency, it was never fully established. He was succeeded by Chin Shu-jen, who unfortunately lacked both his
character and his political sagacity, with the result that the
Province soon relapsed into a state of turbulence which, in

the early 'thirties, crystallized into a three-cornered civil war. The leaders of the opposing factions were: (i) the Tungan general Ma Chung-ying, who invaded the province from Kansu and for a time controlled the whole of South Sinkiang; (ii) General Chang, the commander of Chin's army who had control of the Ili district, and (iii) General Sheng Shih-t'sai, Chang's second-in-command, who seized Urumchi. In the meantime, Chin had fled. There is some evidence that, at first, all three factions received Soviet support. Later, however, it was Sheng Shih-t'sai who was selected as the most promising and with strong support in the shape of aeroplanes and other modern weapons he succeeded in defeating his rivals. Chang committed suicide, Ma, after holding out for some time in the Kashgar district, finally disappeared into Soviet territory. The establishment in 1933 of Sheng Shih-t'sai as Tupan or Governor of the Province was known as the "Great April Revolution," the anniversary of which was celebrated each year throughout the Province until 1942.

From 1933 until 1942 Sinkiang was dominated by Soviet influence. Early resistance by Ma in Kashgar and by the Amir of Khotan, and the Tungan Rebellion which gained temporary success in the south in 1937, provided the only serious opposition. To what extent Sheng was a mere puppet of the Soviet, or to what extent he controlled the affairs of the Province, one can only guess. The fact remains that during that period Sinkiang became a police state on the Soviet model: all outside influence other than Russian was rigorously excluded; no order of the Central Government was obeyed unless it happened to be convenient; Russian civil, military and scientific advisers were employed throughout the Province; trade with the Soviet Union expanded, all trade with India and with Central China was stopped; Islam was ridiculed in the schools, though its teaching was not actually prohibited; the Chinese national emblem was replaced by a six-pointed red star (the Soviet star has five points) on public buildings, flags and the badges of officials; all foreign missionaries were expelled; Indian traders were persecuted, maltreated and deported in large numbers, often in cruel circumstances; the British Consulate-General in Kashgar suffered a rigid boycott.

In 1940–41 it seemed almost certain that Sinkiang would at last become absorbed into Russian Turkestan, an event foretold by Lord Curzon as long ago as 1901. Towards the end of 1942, however, Sheng Shih-t'sai, presumably taking advantage of Russia's preoccupation elsewhere, performed a remarkable *volte-face*. He placed himself under the orders of the Kuomintang, and arrested a large number of his former subordinates. The Russians withdrew, leaving Sinkiang under the effective rule of the Chinese Central Government for the first time since the foundation of the Republic.

The Chinese were still heavily engaged with the Japanese war and they were naturally slow to consolidate their position. Nothing very much seems to have happened until 1944, when Sheng Shih-t'sai was relieved of his post. On 7th November of that year a rebellion broke out in Ili and quickly spread to the two northern districts of Chugachak and Altai. It was, of course, ostensibly a nationalist uprising, but there seems to be little doubt that the rebels received considerable help from outside. They quickly overwhelmed the Chinese garrisons and massacred a large number of Chinese civilians. They marched on Urumchi, and it seemed as though nothing would prevent them from capturing the capital and achieving their declared intention of setting up a "Republic of Eastern Turkestan" comprising the whole province. The Soviet Ambassador in Nanking offered the services of the Soviet Consul-General in Urumchi as a mediator to arrange a settlement between the rebels and the Chinese. The Central Government accepted this offer and sent General Chang Chih-chung, commander of the North-west Mobile Headquarters, to Urumchi to act as governor and to conclude

peace with the rebels. An eleven-point agreement was signed
(January 1946) by both parties. It provided, among other
things, for a considerable measure of self-government for the
native population, popular elections of local officials and for
a reduction in the number of Chinese troops in Sinkiang.
A coalition government was formed, but there was discord
between the two parties and tension developed.

In the meantime, in the autumn of 1945, another revolt
broke out, this time among the nomad population of Sarikol
on the south-western frontier of the Province. There is no
doubt that a considerable number of the so-called rebels
came from across the border, or that the arms and ammunition for the revolt came from the same source. Most of the
small Chinese garrisons were quickly annihilated; some fled
to Gilgit. The "rebels" advanced to the plains, threatened
Kashgar, captured Kaghilik and invested Yarkand. The
position of the Chinese was extremely critical; indeed, it
would almost certainly have been untenable if the rebels had
had the support of the Turki population of the oases. It is
significant that they obtained no help from this quarter, and
that the Chinese forces, which at the time were very weak,
were able to drive them back to the mountains and a year
later to regain control of Sarikol. While the rebels were in
control of the mountain regions they slaughtered and drove
off a large number of cattle, sheep and horses belonging to
their nomad brothers (Kirghiz and Tajik). About this time,
too, Aksu was attacked and portions of the Urumchi–
Kashgar highway occupied from across the Tien Shan.

By the end of 1946 there was an uneasy peace throughout
the Province. In the north each side accused the other of
failure to honour its obligations under the agreement, until
in the summer of 1947 the representatives of the Ili faction
left the capital and returned to Ili, declaring that they would
not co-operate with the Provincial Government until their
demands were met. In the south there was a great deal of
anti-Chinese agitation instigated by communists and

nationalist extremists, probably a very small minority. In the meantime large numbers of troops and a considerable quantity of arms and equipment arrived from Central China, and with these the Chinese strengthened their garrisons in seven out of the ten districts of the Province, to an unprecedented extent. The arrest of a small number of agitators in the south effectively silenced opposition, while in Urumchi and the north-east the Chinese obtained the support of the Khasaks, under their leader Usman, who had quarrelled with the Ili faction.

But by the autumn of 1947 the rift was complete between the Ili faction, who controlled the "Three Areas" (Ili, Chuguchak and Altai), and the Chinese. Notes continued to pass between the leaders of the former and General Chang Chih-chung. The Ili faction took the line that they did not wish to secede from China, and that if only the Chinese would implement their obligations under the agreement of January 1946 they would willingly resume their co-operation in the government of the Province. The Chinese for their part maintained that they had in fact fulfilled all their obligations, that it was the Ili faction who had failed to honour theirs and that it was necessary to maintain a strong Chinese garrison to keep the peace so long as the Ili faction and their supporters in the rest of the Province continued to ferment trouble.

There was no trade and hardly any communication between the "Three Areas" and the rest of the Province. This imposed a severe burden upon the economy of the Province, for, although the south was self-supporting in food, the Urumchi district formerly relied for grain upon the Ili district and was now obliged to import its requirements from Kansu and Szechwan. Nearly all the mineral resources hitherto discovered were in the "Three Areas," whence the wolfram and other products were now exported to the Soviet Union.

Despite all these upsets, China had a fair opportunity of

winning the goodwill and loyalty of the native people of the remaining seven districts, and of restoring a measure of prosperity and, above all, peace to this unfortunate land. Southern Sinkiang, comprising all the great oases around the Takla Makan, is very fertile, well watered from the glaciers of the Tien Shan, Kuen Lun and Pamirs, and underpopulated. Left alone, the people could supply themselves with abundant food; with suitable encouragement, they could produce a substantial grain surplus. Like most agricultural people in similar circumstances, they desire more than anything to be left in peace, a condition they have rarely experienced owing to their unfortunate geographical position. Despite the cries of the nationalists, most of those who thought at all realized that they could not be completely independent of both China and Russia. Ten years of Sheng Shih-t'sai's Soviet-dominated rule gave them a taste of a method of government which they did not like. A small measure of independence, a modicum of social justice, a little less corruption, a genuine effort to improve the educational and medical services, however small its results, would have won whole-hearted and almost universal support. But by the end of 1948 most unbiased observers would have agreed that the Chinese were failing. It must be admitted that they were handicapped by circumstances which may have made their task impossible. The civil war in Central China weakened the confidence of the people and the morale of the officials; economic conditions in the outside world made it impossible to obtain either the technical help or the tools, even for the most elementary development; the currency inflation which after 1942 closely followed that of Central China, though it troubled the agricultural population comparatively little, made it difficult to launch constructive enterprises and encouraged competitive corruption. As already mentioned, the Ili rebellion, which could not fairly be blamed upon the Chinese, and the subsequent separation of the "Three

Areas" from the rest of the Province imposed a severe economic burden and constituted a running political sore. General Chang Chih-chung and many of his able team of senior officers appeared to make a genuine effort to overcome these difficulties and to establish a fair and progressive government. In May 1947, Mahsud Sabri, a Turki, was appointed Governor of the Province; most of the local administrative posts were filled by natives, even though they were often little more than puppets of the local Chinese military commanders. But the Chinese were bad colonizers: with their traditional method of governing minorities by absorbing them, their contempt for what they considered to be inferior races and creeds, backed as it usually was by no evident superiority, their total lack of interest in their work and the country they were working in (there were very few who had bothered to learn the local language, even after a residence of twenty years), their remarkable lack of any civic sense, they were hardly likely to succeed without a rigid dictatorship backed by force and efficiency.

Already by the spring of 1948 there was mounting dissatisfaction. The rising spiral of graft; the burden of the large Chinese army garrisoned in the Province, together with the marriage of Moslem girls with Chinese soldiers; to a smaller extent the complete lack of medical services and economic development and the poverty of education: these were its principal causes.

Such was Sinkiang as I knew it. Now, for better or for worse, a new era has begun, which will certainly change profoundly the pattern of life in that curious, medieval land.

CHAPTER V

KARAKORAM JOURNEY

I

MY second term in Kashgar materialized as suddenly as the first; entirely unexpected and unsolicited. I was in Vienna early in May 1946 when a telegram arrived asking me to take up the appointment again. I had completely lost touch with the situation in Sinkiang, and as I hurried home to learn some more about it and to discuss the proposition with my wife, I was filled with conflicting emotions. The prospect of the journey across the Karakoram and the Pamirs, the thought of being connected again with that strange and lovely land, consumed me with the same tingling excitement as I had felt when planning my first Alpine seasons and when I received the invitation to join my first Himalayan Expedition. On the other hand, the memory of the frustration and sinister hostility I had met with before had a sobering effect. I wondered, too, whether it was fair to ask my wife, for all her love for mountains and strange country, to undertake a prolonged spell of such loneliness and isolation.

The information I got from the India Office was far from promising. The Ili rebellion had thrown Sinkiang into a state of confusion. The so-called "Kirghiz Revolt" in Sarikol had cut both routes between India and Kashgar for the past nine months, and the rebels had advanced to the oases south of Kashgar. Michael Gillett, who had succeeded me in Kashgar in 1942, had been due to leave the previous summer, and though his successor had managed to get through just ahead of the trouble in Sarikol, he himself had been marooned in Kashgar for another winter. He was known to have left for Urumchi in March to travel out by way of

Central China, but nothing was known of his present where-abouts. Nor was there any up-to-date information regarding the situation in Kashgar. Indeed, the outlook was so gloomy that before discussing it with my wife I had almost decided to turn down the offer. She, however, would not hear of my doing so, and we decided to go, whatever the situation. What was perhaps even more remarkable was her readiness to leave our nine-month-old son behind in a nursery school. He was a bit too young to enjoy the Karakoram passes.

In the middle of June, Gillett arrived in London by air from Central China, which he had succeeded in reaching a short while before. Although his account of the situation in Sinkiang was somewhat reassuring, he was not very en-couraging about the prospect of our getting there. Sarikol (Tashkurghan), it seemed, was still in the hands of the rebels, who had extended their operations eastwards to cut the route across the Karakoram Pass from Ladakh. No one seemed to think much of the prospect of obtaining Soviet visas to enable us to travel by way of Tashkent. However, we supposed that if the worst came to the worst, we would be able to get in from Central China as Gillett had got out. We sailed for India from Southampton on 26th July, hoping that by the time we reached Delhi there would be sufficient information available there to enable us to make a decision.

I believe that in travel our feeling for places is influenced very largely by the means of approach. It is one of the curses of modern forms of travel that they deny the traveller the chance to make a slow, progressive mental adjustment to his changing environment, which, in my view, is as necessary to the full appreciation of the place to which he is going as it is to his understanding of the geographical implications of the intervening distance. The faster the means of transportation, the stronger this adverse influence. Thus a journey by air half-way round the world, not only reduces the hemisphere to a series of chromium-plated waiting-rooms and irritating customs officials, but leaves one with a sense of unreality, of flatness, which robs any destination of much of its charm. Whereas even a journey by train, say from Northern India to Ceylon, is slow enough, the change of scene sufficiently gradual, to allow at least a measure of the adaptation necessary for full sensitivity of perception.

Exactly why this should be so I cannot explain. Certainly one would hardly expect an airman alighting upon the summit of a Himalayan peak (if such a thing ever becomes possible) to have the same feelings about it as a mountaineer who has climbed there. But it might be supposed that a sudden change of environment as, say, between London and Peking, should sharpen rather than dull the appreciation of the traveller. I remember once, on the Kamet Expedition, one of my companions said what a pity it was that our return to the flesh-pots would be so gradual that by the time we reached London our appetite for good food and wine, our appreciation of the comforts of civilization, would be so blunted that we would no longer relish them. At the time I agreed with him; but I have since learnt that he was wrong. It is, in fact, only by a gradual return to civilized amenities that one can savour each to the full, or fully enjoy them all.

Whatever the reason, I am sure that my intense enjoyment of Sinkiang and the vivid impression it left upon my mind were due, in no small measure, to the influence of the long journey from India. Not entirely, of course; one would be dull indeed to feel nothing of the subtle charm of its medieval atmosphere, its peculiar beauty, even if one had gone there in a jet air-liner. But without the preliminary experience of weeks of travel with pony or camel caravan across those great ranges, the long absorption in those wide horizons, it would have been harder to throw off all mental contact with the modern world and so to achieve complete receptivity. I was very anxious, therefore, that we should not miss this journey. The approach from Central China would certainly be slow enough, but much of it would have been by mechanized transport.

There are two routes from India to Kashgar. In point of time there is little to choose between them; both involve a march of six or seven weeks from Kashmir, first across the Himalaya, then across the Karakoram range and, finally, across the Kuen Lun or the Pamirs. The western route through Gilgit and Hunza is the one usually taken by travellers. For small caravans it is certainly the easier of the two; the passes are lower and there is some sort of habitation to be found nearly all the way. But the bulk of the trade goes by way of the ancient trade-route, eastward through Ladakh and then north across the Karakoram Pass to Yarkand and Khotan. This is mainly because supplies of fodder for the pack-animals are more plentiful in Ladakh than in Hunza; partly, too, because it would be impossible to take camels along the narrow ledges across the precipices of the Hunza Gorge. It is one of the longest and certainly one of the most remarkable caravan trade-routes in the world. There are two passes of eighteen thousand feet to be crossed and several more of sixteen and seventeen thousand feet. For much of the way the traveller meets with no human habitation of any kind.

When we reached Delhi on 10th August we were disconcerted to find that nothing more was known there of the situation in Sinkiang or of conditions on the trade-routes than the little we had learnt in London. The diplomatic courier service between Gilgit and the Kashgar Consulate was, of course, still closed, and it was assumed that the country to the south of Yarkand and Khotan was still in the hands of the "Kirghiz bandits" as they were officially called. The atmosphere at the Secretariat was depressing. The Calcutta riots were then at their height, and it was feared that similar trouble might break out in Delhi at any moment. All departments of the Government were beset by a mass of problems that clamoured for solution in that delicate period between the end of the war and the granting of independence. Government officials were oppressed by

uncertainty regarding their own futures. It was hardly surprising that the question of how to get a Consul to the
remotest of all their posts did not seem to be one of prime
importance. Someone suggested that a Chinese aircraft
might be chartered to take us from Shanghai to Urumchi. I
had, of course, to acquiesce, though I did so with a sinking
heart. Fortunately, for some reason or other, the proposal
was found to be impracticable.

After we had been there for a few days, however, a telegram came from the British Joint Commissioner in Ladakh
saying that a caravan of Turki traders had left Leh for
Khotan. We decided to follow this bold lead and attempt to
travel by that route. At least, by the time we reached Leh,
in a month's time, we might hope for some definite news
about conditions beyond the ranges. With profound thank-
fulness, but feeling thoroughly jaded, we left Delhi, its heat
and its fevered atmosphere on 20th August and reached
Srinagar in Kashmir two days later. We hired a houseboat
and allowed ourselves a week in which to prepare for the
journey. It was a busy time, but the work was familiar and
congenial and we had leisure enough to enjoy the balm of
our lovely surroundings.

A new Consulate doctor, Allan Mersh, had been appointed
to succeed Doctor Binns, whose relief was long overdue;
he, the new first clerk, Rafaqatullah Khan, and a new compounder, Mohammed Shah, were to accompany us on the
journey. It was arranged that they should travel two days
behind us as far as Leh, to facilitate transport arrangements.

On our arrival at Bombay I had sent a telegram to
Lhakpa's young brother, Gyalgen, in Darjeeling asking him
to come to Kashgar. He had accepted and had reached Delhi
the day before we had left, after some hazardous adventures
in the Calcutta riots. Lhakpa, whom I had left in Kashgar
in 1942, was still there. Gyalgen had been with us on
Everest in 1938 and also on my 1939 Karakoram expedition.
Another contact we had made in Delhi was with my old

Hunza servant, Amir Ali, who had left Kashgar some years before to come to India. In the mysterious manner of Asiatic servants, he had learnt of my reappointment to Kashgar, and, having decided to come with me, I found him, on my first morning in Delhi, waiting for me at the entrance of the External Affairs Department.

Our arrangements were completed on 29th August, and on the following day we went to Sonamarg. We camped in a delightful alp surrounded by fir forest in one of the side-valleys, and spent two pleasant days climbing about the surrounding mountains. On 1st September our caravan assembled and we set out the following morning on the two weeks' march to Leh.

For anyone with a normally sybaritic turn of mind there is, I find, a melancholy complexion about the start of an expedition or a long caravan journey that is difficult at first to combat. With whatever eagerness we may have anticipated it, however much we had craved release from the tiresome restrictions and conventions of normal life, when it comes to the point, the final and irrevocable break with these very conditions bears a sombre aspect. There are so many small things that we take for granted and scarcely notice until, suddenly, they are no longer there. A pint of beer, so easily bought and so lightly appreciated; the comfort of beds, of regular, well-served meals; fresh milk with our tea; access to books, newspapers, letters; the fun of meeting friends—it is always a bit of a shock to find that they have all gone. If it were for the period of a short holiday we would not give the matter another thought, we might even derive a certain masochistic pleasure from their absence. But saying good-bye to them for months, to some of them for years, is a different matter. Only the evening before we had left Srinagar we had dined and danced on the deck of the *Blue Bird,* a houseboat-restaurant run by a Russian who supplied exquisitely cooked Slavonic dishes and excellent wine. To-night our jaded palates would be at the mercy of Gyalgen's

primitive cuisine. It was a sober thought that a month hence
we would still be plodding along, in conditions still more
austere, little more than half our journey accomplished. A
heavy rainstorm overtook us as we reached Baltal that afternoon. It cleared at sundown. Far away to the west, above the
shifting cloud that half-filled the forested valley, a line of
lofty peaks was etched in deep blue against a brilliant sky.
Somehow this lovely sight merely lent poignancy to our
doleful mood.

Fortunately, this nostalgic depression does not last long,
though at the time I never seem to be able to remember that.
As the routine of the march takes a firm hold, so we become
quickly absorbed in it. As our feet become hardened to the
road, our seats to the saddle, our stomachs to camp fare, we
begin to pay more attention to our surroundings. As the
memory of civilized comforts recedes, new animal pleasures
take their place with greater and yet greater zest: the freshness of the morning air, the prodigious appetite at the breakfast halt, the sweetness of spring water after a thirsty stretch,
the bliss of relaxation at the end of the day's march.

On this preliminary march to Leh it was particularly easy
to make the adjustment. There were rest-houses at every
stage, and abundant supplies of fruit, vegetables, eggs and
meat; sometimes even fresh milk. A wide, comfortable path
made walking easy; milestones kept us informed of our progress and of how much more was required of us that day.
Beyond the Zoji La there was an excellent system of transport for touring officials. Word of our coming had been sent
ahead, and at each halt the village headman was responsible
for supplying a fresh set of pack-animals on the day required. Prices were fixed and there was no haggling. The
muleteers, anxious to get their job done, were willing to start
as early as we liked and to travel as fast as they could. Each
morning we rose at half-past five, drank a cup of tea, and
started walking at six o'clock, leaving Gyalgen and Amir Ali
to pack up and get the new caravan under way. Gyalgen,

MELON SELLER   USMAN AKHUN

MONASTERY AT LAMAYURU

mounted on a pony, with the breakfast things packed in a saddle-bag, would catch us up. Between nine and ten, a good half of the day's march done, we would choose some pleasant spot for a halt of two hours. While we were eating our elaborate breakfast of porridge, fried eggs, toast and marmalade and tea, the caravan would pass us, and so reach the next halting-place before us. Most of the daily stages were eighteen miles long; none was more than twenty-two miles. There was little else but pleasure in this luxurious form of travel.

At Baltal we left the forested mountains behind us and saw no more until the following March, when we visited Bostan Terek. For across the Zoji La, we entered the barren ranges of the Indus valley basin. At first the country seemed harsh and bleak after the soft valleys of the Vale of Kashmir, but we were not long in discovering its particular, less obvious charm. I had crossed the Zoji La in 1937 on the Shaksgam Expedition, and knew the route as far as Kargil, whence we had then turned north into Baltistan instead of south-east into Ladakh. Kargil was a typical Balti town. Our first march beyond it was a long one; we passed no important villages and, having dallied on the way, we arrived at Mulbekh late in the evening. It was as though we had stepped straight into Tibet. White- and red-faced buildings, with slightly inward-sloping walls, climbed the hill-side from the wide, fertile valley. Monasteries, gaunt and severe, but incredibly lovely in the evening light, stood upon lofty crags, as though they had grown out of the living rock. There were chortens and "mani" walls along the path. In feature, in speech and in dress, the people were Tibetan.

The Tibetan culture of Ladakh is one of its chief delights. As in Tibet proper, the architecture is in the same perfect harmony with the landscape; the inhabitants have the same attractive characteristics. Whether it is that a religion moulds the character of a people, or whether the native character of the people fashions the religion of their adoption, is a question over which there is much diversity of opinion. If it be the former, then there is certainly much to be said for Tibetan Buddhism. On entering Ladakh we were immediately struck by the cheerfulness of the people, the charming courtesy and friendliness, devoid of all sense of servility, of apprehensive reticence, on the part of men, women and children alike. There was about the country an atmosphere of peace, of mental and material prosperity, of essential goodwill which, after post-war Europe and the passionate turbulence of India, was gently intoxicating.

The way from Mulbekh led over a steep pass to Lamayuru, an oasis of terraced fields and willows cupped in a deep fold of barren mountains, and dominated by the massive walls of the monastery built flush with the sheer cliff upon which it stood. From there we descended into a deep and gloomy canyon, and so emerged into the valley of the River Indus at Khalatse, still three days' march from Leh. The Indus Valley here presents the same appearance of stupendous desolation as everywhere else along its mountain course. As elsewhere, its desolation is relieved, at intervals of half a dozen or a dozen miles, by areas of intensive cultivation. The villages are usually set near the mouth of small, steep, tributary streams, which provide wide alluvial fans on which the terraced fields are built and water easily diverted into irrigation channels. The water of the parent river is rarely used, as it is too difficult to "lift" to the level of the fields. Though Khalatse and the villages beyond were more than nine thousand five hundred feet above sea-level, we found there abundant fruit—apricots, apples and melons; walnuts, too, were just ripening on the massive trees shading the village streets.

Near Leh, the Indus Valley widens out. The southern flank, freed for once from overshadowing precipice, lifts gently to the distant snow-peaks of the Zaskar Range. For once there is natural verdure along the banks of the great river, which flows with unwonted placidity between green meadows and

willow thickets. Here, on 15th September, we found a large
deputation of traders who had come out to meet us. We were
provided with spirited ponies and escorted swiftly over six
miles of sloping desert to Leh, where we found, somewhat to
our embarrassment, that a pompous reception had been
arranged for us. Our arrival apparently was welcomed as a
sure sign that the profitable trade-route to Yarkand and
Kashgar was at last to be reopened. A heavy burden of
responsibility seemed to have descended upon our incompetent shoulders.

Leh is the junction of several important trade-routes;
from Kashmir, from Kulu, from Gartok and the Tibetan
Plateau, from Chinese Turkestan. Like other such junctions
in Central Asia, its bazaar is the meeting-place of many
races: Turkis, Baltis, Kashmiris, Tibetans, Hindus from the
United Provinces, Moslems from the North-West Frontier.
These heterogeneous throngs, their rich and diverse cargoes,
their busy affairs, have had little visible effect upon the placid
life and the distinctive culture of the native people. Leh, the
capital, for all its commercial importance, is still one of the
most typical towns of Ladakh. It is set in a deep recess of the
Indus Valley, a wide bay in the mountains, whose floor slopes
gently up from the river, now some six miles away.
Dominating the town are the monasteries and the huge
palace of the old kings of Ladakh; surrounding it are the
fields, claimed by irrigation out of the desert land, and groves
of willow and poplar; at 11,500 feet above sea-level it is too
high for fruit trees. The wide view over to the Zaskar Range
adds immeasurably to the sense of peace which surrounds it.
There had been wars and strife, and, alas, there have been
since, but we found it hard to imagine that the tranquillity of
this remote and lovely place could ever be disturbed.

The British Joint Commissioner for Ladakh, who was in
residence only during the summer months, had already returned to Srinagar. We had the small Residency and its
garden to ourselves. It was pleasant for a spell to live in com-

fortably furnished rooms and to dine at a table laid with glass and silver. We stayed for a week to prepare for the serious part of the journey.

Of the various trade-routes radiating from Leh, by far the most lucrative was that which led north to Yarkand and Khotan. Silk, felt and rugs came from there; in exchange went a vast assortment of manufactured goods and trinkets. During most of the 'thirties the embargo imposed by Sheng Shi-t'sai's regime upon trade with "imperialist reactionaries" had kept the route closed to traffic. But nearly a decade of hardship and disappointment did not kill the initiative of the traders; and not long after the *volte-face* in Urumchi in 1942–43 caravans again started out across the ancient passes. Then came the "Sarikol revolt" of 1945, and again the route was virtually closed, this time by the presence of hostile forces across it. No one yet knew what was happening on the other side of the ranges. At the end of July a party of bolder spirits had ventured forth, but the majority of the caravan leaders had chosen to wait, though most of them were by now running seriously short of money and supplies. The entire carrying trade was in those days performed by men from Yarkand and Khotan. So when we reached Leh, we found a large number of these Turki traders awaiting our arrival in the naïve belief that our official presence would protect them from the ravages of the "bandits" and ensure a safe passage for their caravans. We had no difficulty therefore in joining up with one of these caravans and hiring as many animals as we required. We even induced them to agree to travel a great deal faster than was customary, and after going over the route again and again we planned a series of stages which would enable us to perform the journey from Leh to Yarkand inside a month. For it was already late in the year and I was anxious to reach Kashgar in time to allow those we were relieving to get back across the passes before winter set in.

The Doctor, Rafaqatullah Khan and Mohammed Shah

arrived two days behind us. Rather to our dismay Mohammed Shah had brought his wife, travelling in strict purdah, and two small children.

We had plenty to do during this week in Leh; repacking our belongings from boxes that had already proved unequal to the rigours of animal transport; laying in fresh stores; buying vast and evil-smelling sheepskin coats and hats against the cold. There were numerous conferences with representatives of the trading community, who had various proposals to make for the development of trade. At least once a day I received a call from a pathetic company of Chinese soldiers, headed by a captain, who a year or so before had escaped to Gilgit from the massacre in Sarikol, and had lately come to Leh in the hope of finding a safe way back to their country. They begged to be taken under our protection. But in spite of all these activities, we found time in the evenings to wander about and see something of Leh.

II

By the afternoon of 20th September all was ready for our departure on the following day. At four o'clock I received an urgent telegram from the Government of India. It stated that a message had been received by Chinese radio from the Consul-General in Kashgar to the effect that the caravan that had left Leh at the end of July had been attacked by "bandits" north of the Karakoram Pass and robbed of both their baggage and their animals. The message recommended most strongly that I should not attempt to travel by that route, but go instead to Gilgit in the hope of travelling through Sarikol. It also said that Dr. Binns and his wife and two children had left Yarkand towards the end of August on their way to Leh in the belief that the route was now safe; and nothing had been heard of them since.

This news put us in an awkward dilemma. It would take us at least three weeks' hard travelling to go from Leh to Gilgit, and perhaps a week to arrange transport for the journey. It was most improbable that we would be able to obtain pack-animals in Gilgit to take us from there to Kashgar, and even if we could it might take us weeks to do so. The journey from Gilgit to Kashgar would take at least another month, so that we would be lucky to get there much before the end of December. Presumably Kashgar had reason to advise me to attempt the Sarikol route, but it seemed that if the "bandits" were operating as far west as the Karakoram Pass, Sarikol, their original base of operations, would be even more dangerous, particularly when the rigours of winter forced them back to more habitable regions. This, too, suggested a potent argument in favour of the Karakoram route. The country beyond the Karakoram Pass was so severe, so totally lacking in grazing and other amenities to support even the tough Kirghiz nomads, that the "bandits" could not remain there indefinitely and there seemed to be a reasonable chance that we could slip through without meeting them, even if they were still molesting the district. Finally, we had already paid some ten thousand rupees to our caravan leaders, and they had already spent most, if not all, of it on fodder and merchandise. It seemed unfair to demand the money back, to say nothing of the "face" we would lose by doing so, and, indeed, by displaying our concern at the news.

On the other hand, to be attacked by bandits in such a place, even if they confined their activities to looting, might have serious consequences. For such a party as ours, to be deprived for example, of pack-animals at 16,000 feet in the middle of October, in country without a stick of fuel, several weeks' march from the nearest habitation, with scores of river crossings, impassable on foot, would be a situation not unlike that of mariners deprived in mid-ocean of their ship. Even the Turki caravan men could hardly be relied upon to walk far carrying loads, to say nothing of the compounder's wife and small children. The "bandits" might be more or less lenient, according to their own plight, though it would certainly be to their advantage to prevent victims from getting through to report their whereabouts and strength. However, it was comforting to reflect that presumably at least some of the unfortunate caravan in question had been allowed to get through or we would not have received the news.

The first thing to do was to talk the matter over with the leaders of our caravan, who, after all, in the matter of property stood to lose a good deal more than we; a fact behind which we might conveniently shelter our pride. We held a solemn conference in the drawing-room of the Residency. The Turkis heard the news with disconcerting calm. They said they would be willing to travel by the Gilgit route if supplies of fodder could be arranged (which was doubtful); but on the whole they thought that there would be less chance of avoiding the "bandits" in Sarikol than across the Karakoram Pass, where the severity of the country, particularly in October, would prevent them from lying in wait for long. But they made it quite clear that they considered it up to me to decide, and that in any case their fate was in the hands of Allah. Such nonchalance might have been comforting, even though it was no guarantee of stoical behaviour in face of an actual crisis; but I was sorry to have the burden of decision thus flung back at me.

I considered the possibility of travelling by a new route far to the west, but it would have been largely through virtually unexplored country, and, even if the caravan men had been willing to try it, which they were not, it would have been altogether too hazardous at that time of year. It happened that Colonel Schomberg had just arrived back in Leh from an exploratory journey in that region. He reported that conditions were already terribly severe on the high plateaux. He agreed that we were more likely to run into trouble in Sarikol than across the Karakoram Pass; indeed, he took a gloomy view of the whole situation and was inclined to think we should return to Delhi.

However, amid all these conflicting considerations, one thing was clear; we could hardly leave the region without finding out what had become of the Binns family. If they had run into trouble, they might be struggling on towards Leh, in desperate need of help. We decided, then, to go forward with the whole caravan as far as Panamik, five days' march away and the last inhabited place on the southern side of the ranges. If all had gone well with them, they should have reached Panamik before we could get there. If not, I planned to leave the rest of the caravan there and go on with a light party by double marches in search of them. The adoption of this plan was a great relief, for although if we ultimately decided to abandon the Karakoram route we would then have to bring the caravan all the way back, thus wasting more precious weeks, at least this final decision was postponed, and action took the place of vacillation.

Consideration of all the many alternatives took a long time and we did not leave Leh until two days later than we had planned. The first obstacle to be crossed was the Khardung Pass, variously estimated on maps at 17,500 feet and 18,200 feet high. It lies in the centre of the cirque of mountains surrounding Leh, and is clearly visible from there. Though the first march was a short one, it impressed upon us the realization that we had left behind the well-ordered comforts of the march to Leh. Despite their two days' grace, the caravan men apparently still had much business to transact; or it may have been reluctance to drag themselves away from the flesh-pots of Leh. Whatever the reason they went on delaying our departure until in a fit of undignified rage I fined them fifty rupees, which I gave to some delighted children among the fascinated crowd assembled in the market-place, and threatened to levy another fifty rupees for every quarter of an hour of further delay. This had the desired effect and the caravan was clattering out of Leh long before the first levy was due. The result was that we did not reach our camping-place, a bleak spot, some 14,000 feet high, at the foot of the pass, until after dark, with all the consequent confusion and misery that implies. This reluctance to start on the day's march proved to be a chronic debility of the Turkis, and during the month that followed it remained an unresolved bone of contention between them and ourselves, and resulted in many late and comfortless camps.

There was a well-graded, zigzag path up the southern side of the Khardung Pass, and despite a late start we were assembled on its snowy crest at eleven o'clock next morning; most of the party suffering from headaches and nausea. Far away to the north, in country with which we were soon to become familiar, we could see the 25,000-foot Saser peaks. The descent from the pass on the northern side was difficult, and the first 500 feet took our caravan about three hours to accomplish. There was virtually no path and the way led over a very steep slope of boulders, close up against the flank of a glacier. The ponies were relieved of their loads, which had to be manhandled over the worst bits, but even so the unfortunate animals slipped and slithered on the icy surface between the boulders in such a way that I expected at any moment to see one of them go crashing down the slope. We did not have anything like enough men to control them. However, we got down without mishap and once in the valley below, the orderly line of march was resumed. Again we did not get in until after dark, but this time we had relatively comfortable quarters in a caravan-serai in the village of Khardung.

Thence the way led down through a narrow gorge, utterly barren except along its narrow floor, where dense willow and tamarisk jungle flanked a stream of sparkling rapids and clear, still pools; and so out on to the huge gravel- and sand-flats of the Shyok River. The Shyok is a tributary of the Indus, which it joins a hundred miles to the west. Like other great rivers of the Karakoram, it flows its wandering course through a trough many miles wide. Almost more than any other feature, these river valleys have impressed upon my imagination the prodigious scale of the ranges which have produced them. For here distance can be realized better than upon the mountains themselves, where movement is restricted and views too wide to be measured by the eye. Here, marching hour after hour, one seems scarcely to move relative to the opposite side of the valley; a buttress by which one has camped is still clearly visible the following evening after a long day's travel.

After a day's march down the Shyok we entered the Nubra Valley, which is almost as large as the former and joins it at such an acute angle that our course was scarcely deflected by entering it. The Nubra River has its origin in, and derives almost all its water from, the Siachen Glacier, which was discovered by Dr. Longstaff in 1909 and, fifty miles long, was thought, until the discovery of the Fedchenko Glacier in the Russian Pamirs in 1926, to be the greatest ice-stream outside Polar regions. Every few miles we passed through villages surrounded by wide areas of irrigated fields. Like those in the Indus Valley, these villages were all situated on alluvial fans at the mouths of side-streams; for, although the precipitation of moisture over the range as a whole must be enormous to maintain the great glaciers, rain- and snow-fall in the lower valleys is negligible and without these glacial streams, cultivation, and thus habitation, would be impossible. Another feature, resulting, I imagine, from the curious fact that precipitation is confined to the vicinity of the high mountains, is the extraordinary form of these side-valleys. Owing to the absence of lateral erosion in their lower reaches, the rivers enter the main valley through slender canyons carved slit-like out of its precipitous flanks. Higher up, these narrow passages gradually expand into wide, open valleys of rich pasture before they finally merge onto the great glacier plateaux above.

We reached Panamik, the last village of any size up the Nubra, on 27th September. To our intense relief we found that Dr. Binns and his family had arrived. They had reached

Panamik on the very same day, and were enjoying the exquisite luxury of being once more in inhabited country, in comparative warmth and comfort, among trees and fields, after weeks of harsh and lonely travel. We listened eagerly to their news. Their caravan had been attacked and fired upon in one of the valleys north of the Karakoram Pass. Although they had not heard of the plunder of the unfortunate trading caravan, they naturally supposed that their assailants were a party of the famous "Kirghiz rebels" or "bandits." They dismounted hurriedly and took cover behind boulders, waved a white handkerchief in token of submission and waited until the shooting stopped and the attackers came up to claim their booty. The shooting continued for a quarter of an hour. Fortunately this was somewhat wild, there were no casualties and none of their animals was hit. When the "enemy" arrived they found that they were a body of Chinese troops who had been sent to the area in search of the "bandits" and had mistaken the caravan for their quarry. The officer-in-charge made scant apology for his mistake and they were left to proceed with their journey.

The Chinese had had some excuse for shooting first and asking questions after. On our way to Panamik we had been overtaken by a special messenger from Leh bringing further news from Kashgar relayed by telegram from Delhi. It had informed us that a body of Chinese troops had been sent (presumably before that encountered by Dr. Binns) to deal with the "bandits," that they had encountered them and had been defeated, losing most of their number. It was reassuring to know that action was being taken against the marauders. Even though it appeared not to have been very successful hitherto, it seemed unlikely that they would remain in the district until stronger forces arrived. So, though with some misgivings, we decided to continue on our journey.

The next day's march took us some sixteen miles farther up the Nubra Valley, to the foot of one of those slit-like side-valleys already mentioned. It would be difficult to imagine a less likely looking place for the continuation of the great trade-route to Chinese Turkestan. It was manifestly impossible to get up the gorge, its floor wholly occupied by a thundering river, its sheer walls almost touching each other a thousand feet above. To the right of its mouth the great precipices continued perpendicular and unbroken; to the left was a vast slab of smooth rock, two thousand feet high, very steep and, apparently from below, not offering a foothold for a goat. As we gazed up at it, however, we gradually detected a tiny black line moving, ant-like, across the slab about half-way up. This was one of the caravans of ponies and camels that had now joined us in our journey, and had made an earlier start from Panamik. It looked like some fantastic conjuring trick, until we realized that a wonderfully well-engineered path had been constructed zigzag up this remarkable place, to turn the gorge and permit access to the valley beyond. From below, this path was almost invisible owing to the steep tilt of the rock.

So far as I know, no one has traced in detail the history of this great trade-route; if this is so, it is probably owing to lack of available information concerning the early pioneers. I had hoped, before writing this book, to attempt to do so, for it would be a fascinating study; or, at least, to make a synthesis of what has been written about it. Unfortunately I have not had the opportunity, nor access to the necessary books. It is difficult to imagine the hardships, the adventures, the repeated failures experienced, many centuries ago, by the original pioneers of the route, in quest of trade or conquest, before they succeeded in finding a way through the labyrinth of gorges, the innumerable blind alleys and across the awful solitude of seemingly endless ranges. In all probability it was not one party of explorers but many, who, during the centuries before the establishment of regular trade, had to find the route for themselves, without any guidance save for the vague knowledge that it had been done. For, unlike the sea pioneers, these explorers probably left no detailed record of their journeys, and certainly no charts to guide their successors. Climbing the Matterhorn to-day, it is hard to appreciate the difficulties and doubts that beset the minds of Whymper and his contemporaries, or, sailing round the Horn, to imagine the terrors it held for the early navigators. So with this trade-route; though the physical conditions of travel are precisely the same as they were a thousand years ago, though there has been little improvement in the "road," familiarity with the way has removed all but the purely objective difficulties and hazards: the problem of keeping the pack-animals alive, blizzards on the great passes, cold, the fording of the rivers, and, in their season, bandits. It is possible, I suppose, even for the new-comer to perform the journey and to notice nothing but the tedium of the marches and the stark discomfort of the country. But to anyone with any geographical sense it must be at least a profoundly impressive experience.

From the top of the great rock slab, more than two thousand feet above the valley floor, we looked back down the Nubra to the isolated patches of trees and cultivation which represented the last signs of permanent habitation we were to see for almost three weeks until we reached the first oases of the Tarim Basin. Then, crossing a shoulder, we were swallowed up in the desolate gorge beyond. By the evening of the second day from Panamik we reached a wide confluence of open valleys surrounded by great ice-peaks, up to twenty-four thousand feet, with many glaciers descending towards us from the saddles between them. On one of these saddles lay the Saser Pass, 17,480 feet high, the next major obstacle in the way. Again it was nearly dark before we started to pitch camp and, as we were above 15,000 feet and a sharp wind was blowing down from the glaciers, it was cold work. We did not descend below that altitude for the next ten days.

The crossing of the Saser Pass is, in many ways, the most

exacting part of the whole journey; certainly for the ponies. In foul weather it is apt to be a hazardous business, and I should hate to be caught in a blizzard with a caravan of ponies high up on the glaciers. On the northward journey, with the animals still fresh and well fed, it is not so bad, but on the journey from Turkestan it comes near the end, when the animals are usually very weak from fatigue, hunger and exposure. This last effort often proves fatal to them even in fine weather, and in the valley leading up to the Pass we first encountered that dismal line of corpses, bleached skeletons and heaps of bones which formed a continuous trail for hundreds of miles until we reached the first oasis beyond the ranges. Indeed, on this account it would be hardly possible to lose the way, and in the absence of any path when we were not marching with the caravan we often found ourselves following this grim trail. Of course, it represents the relics of many decades of caravans. It has been estimated that an average of 15 per cent. of the ponies and camels perish on each journey. Considering the difficulties of the route and the natural temptation to the traders to overload their animals with merchandise at the expense of fodder, I am surprised that the death-rate is so low.

We started comparatively early the next morning. The weather was clear and still. For the first two hours the going was easy along the broad floor of the valley, until we came up against a great semicircle of glaciers at its head. The lower part of the glaciers consisted of a series of ice-cliffs separated by steep ice-falls. The only way through was to the left, up a narrow corridor of moraine, consisting mainly of large boulders, pressed hard up against the precipices of a rock peak. It was the kind of ground on which one spends a large proportion of the time on any mountaineering expedition, but over which I should never before have dreamed of taking pack-animals. It was steep, there was not the least vestige of a path, nor any chance of making one between the boulders, on which the ponies' hooves scraped and slithered agonizingly in their efforts to gain and keep a purchase with trembling, bleeding legs. It was terribly slow work, as each pony required individual attention and there was only one man to every eight animals. As we struggled to get the unfortunate creatures up that moraine, ground so very familiar to me in different circumstances, I had repeatedly to remind myself that I was not on an expedition engaged in a desperate attempt to get pack-transport to a high base camp on a mountain or into a piece of unexplored country, but that I was performing a necessary journey along a regular trade-route to take up a government appointment.

At length we got past the zone of ice-falls and the angle of the glacier to our right became sufficiently gentle for us to take to the ice. Then for the next few miles the going was fairly easy. The ice was hummocky, but no snow lay on it and there were very few crevasses; deep ravines had been cut by surface streams, but these lay more or less parallel with the line of march and caused little inconvenience. The pass itself was on a wide ice-field, so gently rounded that it was difficult to tell when we had reached the actual crest. Beyond, the ice heeled over to form the glaciers on the far side, gradually steepening until, after another two or three miles, we were forced to find a way off it to the left. Thence we descended a small cwm, which led us once more into the valley of the Shyok, 160 miles up-stream from the place where we had crossed it before.

Near the headwaters of the Shyok River is the site of the famous Shyok Ice Dam. This is a typical example of a phenomenon which is fairly common in the Karakoram Range, and its fame is due to the terrible destruction it has caused. Such a dam is formed by a large glacier advancing across a major river valley until the ice presses up against the cliffs on the opposite side. The river thus obstructed forms a great reservoir behind the ice-barrier. When the glacier starts to retreat, perhaps after many years, the barrier is weakened and may burst, releasing the pent-up water in a tremendous flood. The Shyok Dam has formed and burst several times during the past century. Some idea of the immense volume of water involved is shown by the fact that villages were destroyed hundreds of miles below the dam, throughout the course of the Shyok and far down the Indus below the junction, and that floods were caused in the plains of the Punjab some eight hundred miles away as the river flows. The last occasion was in 1929. Warning had been given of the impending catastrophe by travellers and explorers.

The site of the dam was little more than a dozen miles above the point where we reached the Shyok River. I was very anxious to visit it, partly to satisfy my own curiosity and partly so that I could furnish a report upon the state of the glacier and whether the dam had formed again or was likely to do so in the near future; for it had not been visited for a good many years. Our route, however, lay straight across the Shyok and up a nullah into the mountains on the opposite side. So I arranged for the caravan to make a short march on the following day, and set off at six o'clock up the river, together with the Doctor and Gyalgen, mounted on the three best ponies. Our progress was a good deal slower than I had expected. In the first place, we had to ford the river many times, and though by now this had sunk almost to its winter-level, the current was very strong and we had to search carefully for places where it could be crossed. Then, the valley floor was mostly composed either of boulders or of soft sand into which the ponies sank deep, so that we could rarely get them into a trot. Again, there were frequent spurs and outcrops of rock which were difficult to cross.

The valley was fascinating; I think it was the weirdest place I have ever seen. To the right, for mile upon mile, precipices rose straight out of the river-bed for several thousand feet. These were rent by slender, vertical clefts which sometimes united in depth so as to carve

CAMEL CARAVAN

ICE CLIFF ON SASER PASS

TOWARDS THE KARAKORAM PASS

gigantic monoliths, isolated from the main face. The vast walls were slashed across with bizarre colours, like some monstrous oil-painting. To the left the mountains stood well back from the valley. From them, over the steep intervening ground, came a series of glaciers of that peculiar pinnacled formation found to the north of Mount Everest and on the northern side of the Karakoram. The pinnacles, a dazzling white, looked like columns of a ghostly army advancing upon the bastions across the valley. I have never before seen a great river valley so completely sterile, so utterly devoid of any form of vegetation. It was the kind of valley one might expect to find in the exotic landscape of a dead planet. There was no cloud in the sky; the brilliant blue above sharpened every outline, every contrast of shadow and colour. The air was very still. The hiss and boom of the river echoed far up the cliffs; but here and there, by some trick of acoustics, we found ourselves in a pocket of absolute silence. At about two-thirds of the distance we reached a glacier which descended to the floor of the valley. By climbing a small bluff to the side we could see right to its head, which was enclosed by a magnificent cirque of ice-peaks, 22,000 to 24,000 feet high. The sight of their sublime, ordered grandeur was a relief after the grotesque structures, the chaotic desolation of the valley.

It was one o'clock before we reached the site of the Shyok Dam. The glacier, which came down a wide tributary valley from the west, sprawled across the main valley in a tumultuous jumble of ice. But the most advanced ice-cliffs were two or three hundred yards from the cliffs on the opposite side. Moreover, so far as I could judge from the formation of the ice, the glacier was "retreating"; that is to say, the terminal ice was melting faster than the advance of the main body of the glacier could reinforce it. The "advance" and "retreat" of a glacier is normally determined by the excess or deficiency of the snowfall in its collecting basin. In a district where the snowfall is usually just sufficient to maintain

M.T.— 6

the extent of the glaciation, a glacier will "advance" following a cycle of exceptionally heavy precipitation, and "retreat" after a cycle of exceptional drought. But the glaciers of the Karakoram, some at least, behave in a very odd fashion, for which there is as yet, so far as I know, no plausible explanation. I know of several cases where a tributary glacier has been "advancing" rapidly while its neighbour, a couple of miles away, with the same aspect and with a collecting basin in an adjacent corrie of similar size, has been "retreating."

We had no time to spend on a close investigation of the dam, so, after taking a set of photographs, we started back as fast as we could go. We made much better time on the return journey owing to our knowledge of the way and of the best places to ford the river, and at half-past five we reached the little side-valley opposite to our camp of the previous night. It was a narrow gorge flanked by vertical cliffs, but it had a flat, sandy floor and contained only a small stream, so that we could travel at a good speed. After we had gone along it for several miles, the tracks in the sand suddenly ceased. There was an inconspicuous crack in the right-hand wall of the gorge, but at first I could not believe that the way lay there. In the first place, it seemed impossible that it could lead anywhere but into the bowels of the mountain; secondly, it did not look wide enough to admit a pony, let alone a camel. However, the evidence of the tracks was irrefutable; so, dismounting, we led the ponies into it. Inside, the crack, or chimney as it would be called in climbing parlance, became a steep gully, so narrow that in several places the pack-animals must have had to be unloaded to get through between the vertical walls. Again it seemed incredible that we were on a trade-route, and that anyone could have bothered in the first place to search for a route in such an unlikely-looking place. But after half an hour of scrambling we suddenly emerged into a great, open valley, several miles wide, running between two ranges of rocky peaks. The contrast was astonishing, and, but for the tracks and the skeleton trail we might have been at a loss to know which way to turn. The surface was perfect and we coaxed our tired ponies into a canter. It was getting dark when we reached the caravan, encamped below the crest of a gentle pass.

For the next ten days we travelled through the most forbidding country I have ever seen. By now we were far from the great ice-peaks of the Karakoram, and it was only occasionally, crossing a pass or a high plateau, that we saw them in the distance. Their absence increased the appearance of wild desolation in our surroundings. For ice-peaks have shape and majesty; the purity of their outline and their commanding presence dwarf, and so largely obscure, the barren surroundings from which they may rise. Here there was nothing to distract the eye from the stony wastes, the interminable scree slopes, the vast ruins of rock; mountain skeletons, huge, but without form or identity. Considering the great elevation, there was a remarkable absence of glaciation. We passed some glaciers, hideously deformed, blackened with rubbish, coiled like repulsive serpents in their sunless chasms. But in this savage wilderness there was often exquisite beauty; particularly in the early morning and in the evening when the slanting sunlight brought out the delicate colouring in the rocks and subdued the austere landscape to match the simplicity of celestial space.

For three days the way led through gorges, and our view was restricted to our grim surroundings. Then we climbed up on to a wide, flat plateau, 17,000 feet high, known as Depsang; a waterless stony desert, above the rim of which the ice giants of the Siachen appeared shimmering and detached from the earth in a kind of mirage. All this time we were blessed with perfect weather, and, what was more important, there was little or no wind. So during the day we were warm enough, though it was very cold at night; at sundown we used to creep into our sleeping-bags, fully dressed except for our boots, and remain there until the sun was up next morning. It was difficult to estimate distances, but I suppose we normally covered from twenty to twenty-five miles a day, and, occasionally, about thirty, which was as much as the pack-animals could do at that altitude. From the Depsang plateau we descended about a thousand feet to a river known as the Chip Chap, which is the longest head-stream of the Shyok. Crossing this, we entered a valley which led to the Karakoram Pass.

We crossed the Pass, and so from India into Sinkiang, on 6th October. For all its 18,250 feet, and despite its position on the crest of the main watershed of the greatest range on earth, it was a curiously unimpressive affair. It consisted of a gentle, rounded gap, one of many, in the flank of a rounded valley; to our jaded eyes, considerably less spectacular than Sty Head or Pen-y-Pass. When we reached the top, we saw a large caravan approaching up the slope on the other side. This was a welcome sight, for we were now within a day's march of the area where the bandits had been operating, and the presence of the caravan presumably meant that the route was now reasonably safe from this menace. The caravan men were quite as delighted to meet us, for they were unprovided with the necessary visas to enter India. They implored me to give them letters of recommendation to the authorities in Leh. In the circumstances, I had not the heart to re-fuse. Somehow the idea of requiring a visa to cross this howling wilderness seemed absurdly incongruous, and though it was part of my business to enforce this piece of modern barbarism, the rules of hospitality which generally govern the behaviour of people living and travelling in desert places seemed to demand some concession.

We were now in the upper basin of the Yarkand River, and for several days we made our way down this great water-course. Here our main preoccupation was in crossing from side to side of the river, as it flung itself, first against one wall of its valley, then against the other. During the course of one day we had to ford the river as many as thirty times.

Even at this time of year it was quite an alarming business as one's pony, with belly submerged, struggled to maintain a footing on the shifting boulders against the powerful current, whose swirl made one giddy to look at; or perhaps worse still to watch the staggering pack-ponies, with great "bow waves" beating up against our precious belongings on their flanks. In July and August the river is usually quite unfordable, even for camels. One night we spent with a company of Chinese soldiers who had been sent up from Khotan on anti-bandit operations. Farther down the valley, when we had reached the moderate elevation of 12,000 feet, we found little jungles of tamarisk and driftwood washed down by the summer floods which provided us with the novel luxury of camp-fires. We were now barely a week's march away from the basin of the Zug Shaksgam that I had been exploring nine years before, and I spent much of my time speculating how the various side-valleys to the south fitted in with our survey of that well-remembered country.

One morning we left the valley of the Yarkand River for a narrow gorge which led up to the 16,500-foot Yangi Dawan. The gorge was very difficult for the pack-ponies. They kept slipping into crevices or getting themselves and their loads wedged between great boulders and the vertical walls of the gorge, thus causing a traffic block behind them until they could be extricated. The caravan men had been particularly slow in getting away that morning, and it soon became obvious that we would not be able to cross the Pass before nightfall as we had planned. The weather had broken, and when in the late afternoon we eventually emerged from the gorge it started to snow heavily. I had intended to force the caravan on over the Pass even if it took us half the night, in the hope that this would at last teach the men the folly of starting late in the morning. But eventually the sight of the unfortunate compounder's wife sitting with pathetic resignation on her pony, and the thought of probable further casualties among the animals (we had lost two), softened my bad-tempered resolve, and I agreed, with ill grace, to stop for the night a little way below the crest of the Pass. It was a bleak, comfortless spot among the boulders, and once again we were without fuel for our evening meal. I was somewhat mollified by hearing, close at hand, the evening chuckle of ram chikor. While the camp was being pitched, I managed, after an easy stalk under cover of the gathering dusk and the falling snow, to shoot one of these magnificent birds, which gave us promise of a welcome change from tinned food for the next two days.

Beyond the Yangi Dawan we began to feel that we had left the severities of the high range behind. The mountains, though lower, were no less barren and rugged, and some of the gorges just as grim, but in the valleys we found, here and there, delightful willow groves along the river banks, and sometimes wide stretches of pasture, while the climate became so balmy that we shed at least our outer garments before turning in at night. On 16th October we crossed the last pass, a mere 10,000 feet, and on the 17th we found ourselves marching down a hot, waterless valley between low desert hills which formed the last northward spurs of the range. We reached its end and saw, across a stretch of dazzling sand, a dark line of poplars, the first oasis of the Tarim Basin. Two hours later we were lying in the shade of a willow hedge beside a bubbling stream, eating melon after delicious melon, and bunch after bunch of sweet, seedless grapes, as though our thirst and our greed would never be satisfied, while Mohammed Kurban, the caravan leader, was engaged in the tortuous negotiations of an Oriental customs post.

The main part of the journey was over. The past seven weeks, which, because of their full and varied life, had at the time seemed so long, now contracted and telescoped into a single unit of experience. There had been no great hardship, for we had had plenty of food, and were adequately clothed and equipped against the cold. Indeed, once we had accepted the conditions of travel, the time and distance involved, we had found in the simplicity of our daily routine a feeling of peace and of well-being such as perhaps no other form of travel can give. But the slow, plodding progress through a gradually changing scene, the hundreds of miles of uninhabited country, the lonely camps which gave us a sense of kinship with the stark magnificence of our surroundings, had caused us to shed the mental habit of our former life and left us acutely sensitive to the impressions of our new environment.

I had thought that I remembered that country well; I had certainly thought about it enough; but I was astonished at the force with which half-forgotten memories returned: the strange moonlit feel of the landscape induced by sunlight diffused through the dust haze; the way the shadows melted into the mud walls of the houses; the unsubstantial appearance of the loess cliffs; a hundred sensations of sight and sound and smell, too intermingled for distinct analysis. Most of us, I suppose, experience something of the same surprise returning to England after a long spell abroad. However much we may have thought about it, there are still so many things we have forgotten; the greenness of the fields, the scent of a box hedge, the special colour of winter woods, the size of the sheep and cows, the freshness of the air, or the peculiar, rather exciting smell of the Underground Railway.

CHAPTER VI

THE ARCH

SOME twenty-five miles west-north-west of Kashgar is a
small range of jagged rock-peaks. From Kashgar it does
not look very impressive, as it is seen end on and is
partly obscured by a featureless mass of desert hills. But
from the north or south the range, which for want of a better
name we called the Tushuk Tagh (Cave Mountains), is seen
to consist of scores of bold pinnacles stretching in long
ranks from east to west. The highest peaks are probably
about 11,000 feet.

While I was travelling from Kashgar to Tashkent in 1942,
I saw from Min-yol (twenty-five miles west of Kashgar) that
one of the peaks was pierced by a hole which appeared to
extend from a couple of hundred feet below its summit
almost down to its base. From a distance of ten miles it was
difficult to form an idea of the size of this gigantic archway,
but I estimated that the vault could hardly be less than a
thousand feet high.

It was not until several years later that I had an
opportunity of attempting to investigate this remarkable
phenomenon. Greatly under-estimating the difficulty of the
task, my wife and I set out from Kashgar one week-end in
January 1947 with this object in view. We took with us our
two Sherpas, Lhakpa and Gyalgen. A few miles east of
Min-yol we turned off the road and made our way up a
broad water-course which led us in the direction of the
highest peaks. The Arch, now clearly in view, was among
them. For several miles we made our way across a boulder-
strewn desert which sloped gently down from the foot of the
range. It was one of those days, rare in Turkestan, when the

air was crystal clear and the great ice-peaks of the Kashgar Range could be seen in every detail.

Reaching the foot of the range, we climbed a small spur to prospect for a route. From here we could see that the range was divided into two distinct zones. The first was a region of foot-hills composed of shale and sandstone strata which dipped to the north at a general angle of about fifty degrees. Beyond the foot-hills rose the perpendicular rampart of the main peaks, whose clean-cut sides showed, so far as we could see from where we stood, no sign of stratification. A deep canyon ran up into the heart of the foot-hills and we could see that it had several branches. It was obvious, too, that this canyon was only one of a large number of similar passages which, with their branches, split the foot-hills into an intricate labyrinth of gorges. Each of the narrow clefts in the jagged skyline, by which the peaks of the main range were separated from each other, probably represented the continuation of one of the main canyons. The Arch was no longer visible, but we could make a fairly accurate guess at its general direction. Noting that we must take an early branch to the left to maintain this direction, we started up the canyon. It was rather like plunging into a maze after a brief, bird's-eye view of some of its passages.

For a short distance, a broad, flat floor wound between cliffs cut square out of level alluvial deposits. As we entered the foot-hills, the gorge narrowed abruptly, the walls rose to a height of several hundred feet above us, often sheer and sometimes overhanging. The strata, composed of alternating beds of sandstone and shale and variously metamorphosed examples of each, stood out in extravagant relief, dipping at a high and uniform angle. The whole structure appeared alarmingly unstable; an appearance amply confirmed by the frequent masses of landslip debris with which the gorge was choked. The gorge was dry, except here and there where ice, clinging to the walls, marked the position of springs.

We turned up the first branch passage to the left. It was steep, and choked with debris; so steep, indeed, that after a couple of hours' scrambling we found ourselves only a hundred feet below the crest of its confining walls and it showed signs of ending in a fan of shallow cwms. We climbed to the brittle crest of a ridge to see where we were. The surrounding country presented a remarkable appearance. It seemed as though we were standing in the midst of a stormy sea, its crested waves poised to break over the plains to the south. The "wave" on which we stood was one among thousands, each indistinguishable from the rest. The island peaks of the main range appeared no closer; of the Arch there was no sign. To our right we looked down into a deep canyon, which was obviously a continuation of the one we had started up, or a major tributary of it. It had curved round to the north-west since we had left it and now seemed to lead in exactly the right direction. We had obviously been too hasty in our decision to abandon it for its promising but feeble tributary.

When the direction of these valleys was at right angles to the strike of the strata, their sides were almost vertical and frequently overhanging. Although this was their general direction, their sinuous courses placed some portions of them parallel to the strike. The south slope of the valley then followed the angle of dip, often right to the top of the flanking wall. This was the case where we had emerged and we had little difficulty in finding a route down into the canyon. The view which we had seen from the crest of the ridge, though spectacular, was depressing and we realized that we could not hope to reach the foot of the main peaks that day. However, we had time to prospect a bit farther, and we followed up the canyon for another hour or so. On the whole there was no difficulty in doing this, but there was a frequent tendency for bands of comparatively hard strata, less easily eroded than the rest, to form overhanging curtains across our path. Eventually, just as we had reached our self-imposed time-limit, we were confronted by one such curtain over which it was impossible to climb. But here again we were lucky in that it occurred at a place where it was possible to climb out of the bottom of the gorge and along one of its flanks. So we returned to Kashgar confident that we had not yet been baffled by this line of approach.

About a month later we decided to devote another week-end to the problem of reaching the Arch. This time we camped in the mouth of the canyon. We had left Kashgar in a severe dust-storm which continued throughout the journey. Fortunately, the wind was from the north-west and eventually it blew the usual dust haze away, so that by Sunday morning the air was again clear. We breakfasted in the early light and watched the dawn break over the ranges to the south. Framed by the walls of the canyon, Kungur and the great ice-saddle of Chakragil gradually emerged, flooded in the soft sunlight, from the liquid purple shadows of the plains.

We reached the overhanging curtain in little more than two hours and had no difficulty in climbing round it. Beyond, the going was again easy and such glimpses as we had of the peaks showed that we were getting appreciably nearer to them. But soon the floor of the gorge began to steepen; the valley split repeatedly into several branches and it was difficult to decide which to follow. In any case it seemed clear that they would soon peter out and deposit us again like flotsam on an isolated crest in the sea of foot-hills. But this time we emerged on a fairly wide gravel plateau, so far as we had seen, a unique feature in that landscape. At first we naïvely hoped that it might lead us without further trouble to the foot of the peaks, which now seemed much closer. They were a remarkably fine array, rising in smooth unbroken sweeps of prodigious steepness, three or four thousand feet above their foot-hills.

We had not walked more than two hundred yards along the gently sloping plateau before we were brought up on the brink of a sheer drop, down which we looked into the gloomy recesses of another canyon. From its size, structure and direction, it was obviously the main valley of a system entirely separate from the one which we had left; it drained to a point some way farther along the range to the west. At the point where we overlooked it, it was joined by a large tributary canyon which bounded our tableland on the north. It was obvious that before we could progress another yard towards our objective we must climb down into this new system. There was no feasible way of doing this from where we were and we made our way along the brink of the tributary canyon. Soon the tableland gave place to the usual series of wave-like ridges which made progress very laborious. It was a long time before we reached a point from which we could climb down into the gorge.

It was already getting late, so my wife and Lhakpa waited on the ridge while Gyalgen and I climbed down into the canyon as fast as we could. We were now very close to the foot of the main peaks and could see the point where the tributary canyon disappeared into one of the slit-like ravines that split the main massif. But I could not yet see of what rock the peaks were composed. Their smooth faces and the apparent absence of stratification suggested a massive limestone, though the boulders in the gorges contained a large proportion of crystalline rock as well as of limestone. We made our way down to the junction and turned up the main canyon. Here we found thickets of tamarisk, briars and coarse grass, watered by a stream which was only partly frozen. We raced along the almost level floor. But before we had gone for half an hour from the junction the walls of the canyon converged above us and we entered a circular cavern. The floor was covered with a sheet of ice; at the far end a frozen waterfall, about sixteen feet high, hung from a V-shaped cleft which represented the continuation of the gorge. Supported by Gyalgen on its lower portion I cut steps up the waterfall, climbed through the cleft and emerged on to a second recess, also floored with ice, but this time open to the sky. A second frozen waterfall a good deal higher than the first confronted me. I did not attempt to climb it, and doubt if I could have done so if I had tried. A jutting stratum of rock which formed part of the roof of the lower recess, sloped back along the wall of the canyon at the prevalent angle of about fifty degrees. It was formed of hard conglomerate and was easy to climb. It took me right to the top of the 300-foot wall and once more I looked across that incredible tangle of sharp ridges that formed the foot-hills. There was no obvious way of climbing on towards the peaks nor of regaining the floor of the canyon above the second waterfall, but I did not make a thorough search as it was already an hour later than the time I had decided to turn back.

It was the middle of April when we made a third attempt to find the Arch. This time we went to the village of Min-yol, where we consulted the local population. In my experience, Asiatic peasants are usually quite uninterested in the natural phenomena around their homes, unless they happen to have some economic significance; the most majestic mountain is left unnamed; the advance of a glacier will pass unnoticed unless it should happen to destroy their houses or encroach upon their grazing-grounds. We were surprised to find, therefore, that the villagers of Min-yol took the keenest interest in the Arch. They and their fathers before them had explored the labyrinth of gorges that led through the foot-hills usually in quest of game, but often, during the perennial revolutions and civil wars that sweep this unfortunate country, when it provided them with welcome refuge from the storm. Never had anyone seen the Arch from close to, let alone reached it. Its curious disappearance as soon as one reached the foot-hills had long been remarked upon, and some of the more adventurous spirits had even set out to find it. The circumstance was fertile for legend. It was said that somewhere among the lofty pinnacles there was a beautiful garden of flowers and fruit trees, inaccessible to the ordinary mortal.

It had occurred to us that the Arch might prove to be an optical illusion. But we had studied it very carefully with a telescope, from various points along the road and from a distance of twenty-five miles to the south, and were positive that it did exist. Moreover, we had seen a similar, though less spectacular, arch above the Artush plain at the eastern end of the range. We had no difficulty in persuading two of the villagers to join in our quest, though they were quite confident that it would not succeed. One of them, Usman Akhun by name, was obviously the J. A. Carrel of the village. He had a splendid physique and the easy rhythmical movements and self-assurance of an Alpine guide.

We set out across the desert to the north. This time the weather was more normal, and a thick dust haze obscured the mountains until we were within a mile of the foot-hills. Then the peaks began to appear in ghostly outline; there once again was the Arch. We entered a canyon which at first I thought was the one that Gyalgen and I had reached on the previous occasion. But it soon became obvious that it belonged to a different system, probably the next to the west. We camped about two miles up the gorge, and set out again next morning at a quarter-past seven. We soon came across fresh tracks of ibex, which had descended from their crags for their morning drink at the intermittent springs on the floor of the canyon. We would certainly have surprised some of the creatures had it not been for the loud and continuous chatter of our guides echoing far up the surrounding cliffs. After about an hour, still following the game-tracks, we turned up a steep side-nullah to the right, intending to continue the exploration of the main canyon later. Very soon the nullah ended in a little cwm surrounded by vertical cliffs. A small terrace ran diagonally across the right-hand wall. We climbed this to the outer edge of the cwm, and round the corner we found that it continued across a big south-facing buttress. It was an impressive place and commanded a fine view over the foot-hills. There were large deposits of ibex droppings, and here and there those of ram chikor. Soon after we had turned the corner, two of these birds came sailing over our heads from the opposite side of the main canyon. We made our way along the terrace for about half a mile, hoping to find some way round the vertical cliffs above. Eventually, however, it petered out high above a system of gorges, which was evidently the one which Gyalgen and I had reached on the previous occasion. There seemed to be no way of getting down into this from where we stood, so we began to retrace our steps.

A couple of hundred yards back along the terrace the wall above was cleft by a crack which, higher up, widened into a chimney which in turn ended under an overhanging block. A suggestion of mine that we might try to climb this cleft was turned down peremptorily by Usman Akhun, who had hitherto nursed the party along like a guide with a bunch of incompetent tourists. I ignored his protests, however, and tying myself on to the end of our 100-foot rope, started to climb the crack. This was obviously regarded as a piece of gross impertinence and but for Gyalgen I think Usman would have pulled me down again. The chimney was not particularly difficult and just as I had run out the length of the rope I reached a wide recess below the overhang. Usman Akhun's blood was up. He removed his boots and started up after me. He was a good climber on slabs, being quite fearless and very agile; but though he managed the lower crack the idea of backing up a chimney was evidently new to him and he could make nothing of it. He struggled valiantly for some time before he was forced to bury his pride and clutch the rope. By this he managed to haul himself up to the recess, where he arrived, winded and obviously impressed.

It was decided that the others would remain on the terrace and await our return. We did not expect that to be long delayed. The overhanging block was pierced by a hole, through which we climbed and so emerged at the top of the cliff. Following the uniform structure of the foot-hills the ground beyond dipped steeply down into a wide notch, beyond which was another formidable cliff. But by following the exposed strata diagonally to the right we climbed down about four hundred feet to the floor of the canyon beyond. Here I found that we had at last penetrated through the foot-hill zone and were right up against the walls of the main massif. I was astonished to find that these cliffs, which stretched in almost vertical sweeps for thousands of feet above our heads, were composed entirely of conglomerate. Although, looking at the smooth faces of the peaks as a whole, there appeared no sign of any bedding planes, examination of the sides of the ravines by which they were cleft showed that the strata dipped to the north more or less in conformity with that of the foot-hills.

We made our way along the canyon. The floor where we reached it was about ten yards wide. Presently it plunged into the vertical wall of the main massif. Here it had a maximum width of about three yards, though often it was so narrow that we had to edge along sideways. For a long way the floor was flat and though it was often deeply covered with snow we could get along rapidly. Usually the skyline above us was so narrow that we could see nothing but the ravine; but sometimes it widened sufficiently to enable us to see, far above, a great amphitheatre of peaks that we were entering. It was obvious that this fantastic passage could not go on indefinitely without interruption. After surmounting two small steps in the floor, we reached a third, about twenty feet high. I managed to chimney up this and went on alone. About a hundred yards farther on the walls of the ravine began to close above me, the light faded and I was soon in complete darkness. Eventually my groping hands came up against a cold slippery surface. I struck a match and saw that a great column of ice descending from the darkness above marked the end of the ravine; at least, so far as I was

TUSHUK TAGH : SOUTHERN BUTTRESSES

TUSHUK TAGH : ENTRANCE TO ONE OF THE SOUTHERN CANYONS

concerned, for I did not contemplate climbing the vertical ice in the dark. I estimated that I reached a point directly below the wall of the amphitheatre.

When I got back to Usman he showed me, with some display of excitement, a number of dead leaves which he had found on the floor of the ravine. He evidently regarded them as indisputable proof of the existence of the legendary fruit gardens, and he preserved them carefully in his hat. We made our way back along the ravine until we reached the point where it widened out at the junction of the main massif and the foot-hill zone. From here we followed another passage, which climbed steeply along the line of junction to the west and led us into a wide cwm filled with tall grass and briar trees. As we emerged into the cwm, we startled a pair of ibex, which bounded up a sloping ledge to the left and stood gazing down at us, silhouetted against the sky. Beyond the cwm a line of overhanging cliffs once more barred our way and effectively disposed of yet one more line of approach.

It was now high time to retreat. Usman was strongly opposed to going back by the way we had come as he did not like the idea of climbing down the chimney. He had no faith in the rope. He argued that we could find a way of traversing across to the terrace where we had left the rest of the party. I was rather doubtful, but the possibility of avoiding some upward climbing was attractive: we had been going extremely fast and I had become uncomfortably parched. A little way below the point where we had entered the canyon we managed to climb on to a ledge which looked as if it might serve our purpose. For some way all went well; but then it began to narrow rapidly and soon it ended above a twelve-foot drop to a parallel ledge below. Usman proceeded to jump down this without much apparent consideration either of the unpleasant landing or of the consequences of thus cutting off our retreat. I was shamed into following suit, though I would very much have preferred to turn back.

Our new ledge took us on for barely a hundred yards before it too ended. This time the drop to the next ledge was more like fifty feet. I was relieved that my companion showed no inclination to leap down this, though at first there was no obvious way of climbing down, nor was there any means of *abseilling*. I began to feel rather foolish, until a few yards back along the ledge we discovered a diagonal scoop down which it was possible to climb. We rejoined our companions on the terrace at about half-past two, about four hours after leaving them for a tentative reconnaissance up the chimney. The melon, without which no one in this country is suitably equipped for travel and which is a very passable substitute for a pint of beer, tasted uncommonly sweet.

We had now seen and heard enough to realize that the chances of reaching the Arch from the south were extremely slight. We had already had several views of the range from among the foot-hills of the Tien Shan to the north, but had seen no sign of the Arch. Nor had any of the Kirghiz nomads of that district from whom we had made enquiries ever heard of it. Nevertheless, we decided to explore the range from that direction, and some weeks later we camped among its northern foot-hills. The weather was stormy. A good deal of rain had fallen and we had some doubts about the wisdom of penetrating those unstable gorges when the hills were wet. Fortunately, we found that, owing to the continued northerly dip of the strata, the canyons did not develop until the hard conglomerate of the main range had been reached. This, too, made the approach considerably easier. Wide water-courses led gently up through low hills to the very foot of the peaks.

But a close view of the range was far from promising. Individually the peaks were not so spectacular as they had been from the south. But from here, there seemed to be several parallel ranges, each with countless jagged summits. It was easy to see why the Arch was not visible from the north. The shape of the skyline bore no resemblance to the one we had seen from the south, which we had taken particular care to memorize. We could not now be certain even which was the highest peak of the range, which had seemed so obvious from there. The maze of ravines by which the range was split was correspondingly complex. It looked as though we would have to devote many more long week-ends to a systematic exploration before we could hope to find a way through to the Arch.

We chose a point on the crest of the range which seemed most likely to correspond to the place where we had seen the Arch, and selected a ravine that seemed most likely to lead in the direction of that point. We were immediately swallowed up in the twisting labyrinth, where we had no choice of direction save where our chosen passage-way divided. The walls and spires above us, though composed of the same hard conglomerate, were quite different in appearance from those we had seen on the south side of the main range. In place of the smooth, almost polished surfaces, the faces here were deeply pitted and honeycombed so that the peaks often resembled gigantic beehives; some were carved into remarkable fretwork patterns; all were excessively steep.

The going was considerably easier than anything we had met on the south side of the range. Mostly the floor of the canyon sloped gently upwards and when it was interrupted by steps, these were comparatively low and easy to climb. This difference was, of course, again due to the northerly dip of the strata. We were making height steadily, and we began to hope that at least we might reach the watershed and be able to look down into the amazing country to the south. A variety of large shrubs grew among the mounds of scree, particularly at the valley junctions, and higher up we were surprised to find a number of small firs. The floor of the ravine was generally about twelve feet wide, though for short stretches it would narrow to about two feet.

At last, emerging from one of these clefts, we were confronted with a sight that made us gasp with surprise and excitement. The gorge widened into a valley which ended a quarter of a mile away in a grassy slope leading to a U-shaped col. Above and beyond the col stood a curtain of rock, pierced by a graceful arch. Through the arch we could see nothing but the clouds of a stormy sky. This sudden end of our search was almost an anticlimax. My wife remarked upon the amazing chance that had led us to choose exactly the right canyon, and at each branch the right alternative so that we came direct to our objective at the first essay. I preferred to think of it as the result of sound mountaineering instinct! We hurried up to the col. There was nothing of an anticlimax about the Arch itself, or the view beyond.

Before we reached the col we had seen only a very small portion of the Arch; now the whole vast structure opened before us. On the other side of the col the ground dropped vertically into a profound abyss, so narrow in its lower portion that its floor was for the most part invisible. The Arch was about a hundred and fifty feet from where we stood, a quarter of its height above us, three quarters below. Its supports, beautifully curved in their upper portion, smooth and vertical below and for a long way down, stood out in sharp relief from the sides of the canyon with which they eventually merged. It was impossible to estimate its total height, but I do not believe that this was far short of a thousand feet. Its span was about one-sixth of its height. The canyon was no ordinary product of fluvial erosion. It looked more like a rift caused by some titanic earthquake. And yet the vast blocks by which it was enclosed had a strange symmetry; for all the incredible confusion of the whole, each feature was clean-cut, sweeping and without blemish; below the walls were some slender buttresses slanting this way and that, quite irrelevant but smoothly curved. It was like some wild design of modern sculpture. A mile away the canyon was blocked by a massive tower of similar form. Probably this was one of the line of peaks whose outer edge we had reached from the south. To pass it on either side or in either direction looked impossible.

A cold wind blew and for the most part the sky was over-cast, though an occasional shaft of sun would light up part of the strange scene before us. With some difficulty we climbed a small peak above the col, from which we saw beyond the canyon into another, scarcely less remarkable than its neighbour.

The next morning, before starting back to Kashgar, we followed another gorge, and again, though with considerably more difficulty, succeeded in reaching the watershed at a minor peak, some 10,500 feet high. The storm had passed, and though the wind was still strong, the air was very clear. The same terrific rockscape lay to the south at our feet, again enclosed by an outer line of towers. Beyond stood the great peaks of the Pamirs looking incredibly high and sharp. Northward, across a wide expanse of desert hills, red and gold, the western ranges of the Tien Shan were arranged in a vast arc, mauve below, dazzling white above in their mantle of freshly fallen snow.

CHAPTER VII

MUZTAGH ATA

THE literal meaning of "Muztagh Ata" is "Ice-mountain Father." It is said that the mountain received its name in the following way: When Sven Hedin asked one of the Kirghiz nomads in the district what it was called, he received the polite reply: "It is called 'Muztagh,' Father." I was told this by one of the former Swedish missionaries in Kashgar, who may have got it either from Hedin himself or from a member of one of his later expeditions. I cannot vouch for the story and I am not even sure whether it was Sven Hedin who was originally responsible for the adoption of the name. However, it is not an improbable explanation of the fact that no inhabitant of Sinkiang with whom I have discussed the matter has ever heard of the name Muztagh Ata. On the other hand, every ice-mountain or range of mountains that I have approached in South Sinkiang is known to the people in its vicinity as Muztagh. As applied to mountains, such names as Kungur and Chakragil, so well known to European travellers, are quite unknown locally. Usually, too, the nearest grazing-grounds to the glaciers of a particular range are known locally as Muztagh. The result has been the adoption by western geographers of the name Muztagh for at least four of the major peaks of Central Asia and for scores of rivers and grazing-grounds. There have been determined attempts by some influential geographers to change the name of the Karakoram Range to "Muztagh." I am glad that these were resisted successfully. The name Muztagh is in danger of becoming a bit overworked, while the name Karakoram, however unsuitable (it means "Black Rock"), has a fine classical ring about it.

For a long time it was thought that Muztagh Ata was the highest mountain in this part of Central Asia. Sven Hedin makes much of this supposed supremacy in his many flowery passages. "Mus-tagh-ata," he writes (*Through Asia,* page 217, published in 1899), "the loftiest mountain in the Pamirs, towers up to the height of 25,600 feet. . . . The unchallenged pre-eminence of Mus-tagh-ata over the peaks which cluster around it is proved by its name, which means 'Father of the Ice Mountains.' " I find it puzzling to account for this confident assumption. A few miles to the north, though entirely detached from it, there lies the huge massif of Kungur. Standing between the two, it is difficult to see how anyone could question the superiority of the latter in height. Even assuming a strong prejudice in favour of the former, it is impossible to account for the use of the phrase "unchallenged pre-eminence," a phrase, more-over, that has not merely been allowed to slip out in the exuberance of descriptive emotion; it is reinforced over and over again in succeeding chapters by the expression of simi-lar sentiments. Apart from the obvious height of several of the peaks of the Kungur massif, the quite exceptional extent of its glaciation would inform any experienced observer that Kungur was among the highest mountains of the world. One possible explanation of the mistake is suggested by the height quoted by Hedin, 25,600 feet. Kungur, whose height is now accepted at about 25,200 feet, must have been observed and its height computed by many travellers in the plains of Kashgar during the nineteenth century. Anyone who asked from the natives what the mountain was called would naturally be given the name "Muztagh." But to accept this explanation merely confronts one with a question still more baffling. How anyone who has seen Muztagh Ata could ever mistake Kungur for the same mountain is quite beyond comprehension. Aside from the fact that they lie twenty-five miles apart, Kungur is a part of a range com-parable with Kangchenjunga, while Muztagh Ata is an isolated peak somewhat resembling a volcanic cone in appearance.

A rare opportunity came my way in the summer of 1947. Bill Tilman joined the Swiss Expedition to attempt Rakaposhi, and I managed to persuade him to come up and visit us in Kashgar before returning home. The Chinese Government kindly granted him a visa to do so. The war had interrupted an excellent habit we had formed during the 'thirties of travelling together. As the years lengthened towards a decade, I had begun to suppose that the thread had been irrevocably broken, and that this easy and profitable partnership belonged only to the past. The prospect of renewing it, even for a brief spell, in a field of such unlimited scope was very exciting. I did not even need to take more than a few days' holiday. I had several just reasons for visiting Sarikol. The various alternative routes to that place led past a hundred unclimbed peaks and a score of unexplored valleys. In Sinkiang a consul is still in the happy position of having to tour much of his district on horseback; even a short tour takes several weeks to complete, so that a few days spent wandering off the route is neither here nor there. It is easy to combine a modicum of business with a great deal of pleasure. We arranged to meet at Tashkurghan on 6th August.

My wife, Gyalgen and I left Kashgar on 28th July. Three days before, I had a severe attack of influenza from which I had barely recovered by the time we reached Tashkurghan. This was a bad beginning. We travelled by the eastern route, by way of Yangi Hisar and the Chichilik Pass, reaching Tashkurghan on 5th August. I had not been there since the occasion of my first arrival in Sinkiang, seven years before, and the place held unpleasant memories for me. Our reception this time was in striking contrast. As soon as we emerged from the mountains we were met by Fatih Ali Khan, the supervisor of our diplomatic courier service to Gilgit, together with all the chief civil and military officials of the place, with whom he was on the best of terms. We were provided with fresh ponies and rode with this impressive escort for the last dozen miles to Tashkurghan, where we were received with lavish hospitality.

Bill arrived on the following day as arranged. We had a dozen alternative plans to choose from. There were, for example, two extremely attractive peaks, twenty or twenty-one thousand feet high, both within ten miles of Tash-kurghan. They were made of solid gneiss, decorated with finely chiselled ice-âretes and precipitous ice-falls; to climb either would clearly call for all the mountaineering skill that remained to us after so many lean years. We could thread our way back to the north through the Shiwakte group, con-necting up some of its unexplored valleys by passes yet to be found. There was the unexplored valley which apparently leads right up into the heart of the Muztagh Ata massif from the south. The east face of Kungur has not yet been seen by Western eyes.

Our choice was unimaginative, and actuated, I think, by second-rate motives. We both had a sneaking desire to see how we would react to high altitudes after an interval of nine years; we both, I suspect, nursed a secret hope to achieve an easy and spectacular triumph. The western route to Kashgar passes close under the western side of Muztagh Ata. This side of the mountain had been explored by Sven Hedin and it was obvious that there was the probability here of a fairly easy route to the top. We ignored a lesson that we had learnt a dozen years before; that to climb a mountain for its height and fame alone is infinitely less rewarding than to attempt a peak whose form has charmed, or to cast a new light upon an attractive mountain range. We agreed that Muztagh Ata from the west had little to recommend it either in interest or beauty; but we chose it first from among a score of others.

But there was a second item on our programme. Two or three marches north of Muztagh Ata, at the point where it plunges into the Gez defile, the western route to Kashgar passes close to the southern side of Chakragil. Though a mere twenty-two thousand feet, Chakragil forms one of the most beautiful sections of the tremendous panorama of snow mountains seen from Kashgar. During two years of exasperating confinement I had drawn solace from the contemplation of its fluted ice-ridges, glistening in the early morning sun, floating high above dark storm-clouds or silhouetted against the evening sky. With Kungur and the others, it greeted me when I returned four years later. I had the exquisite excitement of introducing it to my wife, and it had formed a background of our morning walks, winter duck-shoots and week-end expeditions. We had paid it a brief visit the previous May, and had camped for three days among the pine forests and the wide grassy alps at its northern foot. Now there was the chance of getting on intimate terms with this lovely mountain by attempting to climb it from the south.

We left Tashkurghan on 8th August accompanied by a large cavalcade of civil and military officials belonging to the post. As usual it was taken as an occasion for a wild display of horsemanship in which we took as little part as our mounts would allow. Beyond the five miles which etiquette required our hosts to accompany us, our escort was reduced to two armed Tajik policemen and two junior civil officials. They were sent for our protection and guidance by the Commandant and the Magistrate. These escorts were one of the bugbears of our official tours in Sinkiang and we used to spend much of our time trying to avoid them. The simple policemen or soldiers were fairly innocuous as a rule and could generally be induced to adapt themselves to our primitive taste in travel. But the civil officials were very tiresome. In the first place, they regarded all journeys as evils to be got over as soon as possible. They tried, usually successfully, to exercise dictatorial powers over our every action; they chose our halting-places during the march; there was a fuss every time we decided to walk rather than ride; they stubbornly opposed our choice of camping-sites and forced us to impose upon local hospitality; any divergence from the regular route was, of course, bitterly resented.

There had been a thick dust haze over the country for the past two days, and as we made our way up the wide Tagharma valley we saw little of our surroundings. The dust haze often persists for weeks at a time, even among the high mountains, and can utterly ruin the enjoyment of a journey. It is far more exasperating than bad weather, which, though it may obscure the hills and interfere with plans, rarely reduces the scene to one of such monotony and, indeed, often provides some of the most spectacular views. However, the haze had disappeared by the morning of the 9th, and as we made our way round the south-western flanks of the Muztagh Ata massif the mountains were clear.

The quarter-inch map, No. 42 N. of the Survey of India, marks two points, 22,956 feet and 22,240 feet, on a long ridge running gently down to the south from the summit of Muztagh Ata. Actually these two points are entirely separate peaks, isolated from the main mountain and from each other by gaps several thousand feet deep. There is a similar col between Muztagh Ata (24,388 feet) and a northern summit which is indicated on the map by a 24,000-foot contour ring. From each of these two summits a broad, unbroken ridge descends to the west, separated by a deep trough containing the Yam-bulak Glacier. On his first and second attempts on Muztagh Ata in 1894, Sven Hedin chose the northern of these two ridges. This is surprising, because, although it is the easier of the two, the descent to the col from the northern summit would be a laborious business, while to climb to the main summit from the col would, even by modern standards, be very difficult, if not impossible. On the second occasion, Hedin estimated the highest point he reached at 20,600 feet.

For his third attempt Hedin chose the other ridge, that

comes down from the main peak. He reached a height of 18,500 feet. "Evening was coming on," he writes, "and I was again constrained to beat a retreat, for it would have been useless to wait till the next day and then try to find another passage" (through the crevasses). "It was plainly impossible to venture upon Mus-tagh-ata from this side without special appliances, which were not at our disposal. Above us towered the loftiest summit of the mountain, and down its precipitous sides glided the eternal ice, streaming in part to the collecting basin of the glacier; and where declivities were convex and the ice-mantle was checked by the relief of the underlying ground, it built itself up into veritable terraces, walls, towers and solid blocks of enormous dimensions. To get past these seemed, so far as we could judge from the spot where we stood, altogether beyond the reach of human power." The ice may have changed a great deal in the last fifty years; even so, I am inclined to think that this last sentence was a considerable exaggeration. Nevertheless, it is not surprising that he did not persist, seeing that he had not even a rope. The remarkable thing is that he attempted the mountain at all "without special appliances."

He made a fourth attempt (16th August, 1894), this time reverting to the northern ridge which leads to the northern or lower peak. He camped at the highest point he had reached before (20,600 feet), but did not proceed farther on account of a strong wind. In July 1900 Sir Aurel Stein ascended this same ridge to 20,000 feet. On the previous day his two Hunza "guides" had reconnoitred the ridge to a point about 1,500 feet higher and had found the way barred by a difficult notch.

We made a longer march than we had intended on 9th August, and for a very unusual reason; our transport ponies went so fast and so far ahead of us that we could not catch them up in time to prevent them crossing the Ulugh Rabat Pass, which we had intended to cross the following day. We followed wearily behind and reached the

Pass about sunset. A great mass of dark cloud, streaked with deep crimson, hung over the Kungur massif, beneath which the lower fringes of its vast ice-cap showed cold and gloomy. The rest of the world was flooded in a delicate mauve light. We camped in the wide alluvial plain beyond the Pass.

We were now due west of Muztagh Ata and in full view of the mountain, so that we could lay our plans for climbing it. Without much hesitation we chose the ridge forming the southern flank of the Yam-bulak Glacier, and leading direct to the summit. The alternative was the parallel ridge leading to the minor northerly peak. Before we had seen the western side of the mountain, I had assumed, from Hedin's description, that this would be the best route to follow, partly because it seemed to offer the possibility of using local transport up to a considerable height and partly because it avoided the tangled ice-fall of which he had given such a lurid account. But one look at the face of the mountain overlooking the northern peak was enough to dispel this idea.

The next morning we moved up to a grazing-ground known as Yam-bulak, near the foot of the mountain. Most of the Kirghiz had already moved down to lower pastures, but one family remained. They had intended to go down the following day, but they kindly volunteered to stay while we were there to supply us with milk, cream and butter. The Kirghiz, of course, had little interest in the rapidly inflating Chinese currency. For this reason we used always to travel with a sufficient supply of tea, cloth, rice, soap and mirrors to distribute among them. Not that they ever expected any payment for their liberal hospitality, and they were always overcome with a gratitude out of all proportion to the value of the gifts. We managed to get rid of our escort, who, seeing that we could not be shaken from our incomprehensible intention of going up on to the glacier, shrugged their shoulders and left us with evident relief.

Our hosts provided us with a yak and a driver. We hoped that the beast would carry our loads to a point on the ridge, about 17,500 feet high, where the rock disappeared under the ice and where we proposed to put our first camp. Sven Hedin had taken yaks to considerable heights on the mountain on each of his attempts. He had never had any trouble with them except when he took them on to the ice. Load-carrying was our principal worry. I had not done any since 1939; Gyalgen had done very little during the last few years and none at all for more than a year; Bill had had some practice that summer, but nothing like enough to get back to a reasonable degree of proficiency. Going unladen to 17,500 feet would certainly be a great help, though we did not relish the prospect of carrying all our stuff beyond that unaided, particularly if the snow proved to be bad. We had no spare boots, so that we could not recruit local help for work on the ice; but even if we had, I do not think we could have induced any of the Kirghiz to come with us. In all, allowing for bad snow conditions, we planned to have three camps on the mountain to get us within striking distance of the summit.

We started from Yam-bulak at eight o'clock the next morning (11th). My wife came with us and we also took a Turki youth, Roza Beg, whom we had brought from Kashgar, so as to accompany her on the way back from our first camp. About an hour's walk to the south took us to the Yam-bulak Glacier. It was very broken and be-pinnacled throughout most of its length, particularly in its lower reaches, so that to cross the valley we had to keep below its snout. From there, another hour's easy climbing took us to the foot of the ridge, at about 15,000 feet.

The ridge was a very broad affair and throughout most of its length offered a variety of routes. For the first 2,500 feet it presented a rock slope set at an ideal angle, divided by two deep gullies which contained ice on their upper portions. Once on the mountain we had no means of gauging our height except for Hedin's estimate of the point where the rock of the ridge disappeared under the ice. We were very careful to note our climbing time, so as to reach as accurate an estimate as possible of our vertical progress by dead reckoning. We climbed steadily at a good 1,500 feet an hour, for spells of half an hour each. From the outset the yak made very heavy weather of it, despite energetic exhortations by Gyalgen, Roza Beg and the driver. By the time we had completed our second half-hour spell, we had left them far behind, out of sight. We waited for an hour, and then Bill and I went down to see what was happening. We found that the yak had given up about five hundred feet below, and the driver was lying on his face gasping out the information that he himself was dying. Evidently yaks are not what they were in Sven Hedin's day. We divided up the loads and plodded back up the slope, whereupon the driver revised his plans and set off down at a brisk speed. My wife insisted on carrying some of the baggage, which noble gesture I did not resist too strongly.

At about a quarter-past three we reached the end of the rocks. My wife and Roza Beg went down, while we pitched our tent and brewed tea. Later in the evening, Bill and I went forward to reconnoitre. The rock disappeared immediately under a moderately steep ice-slope which obscured the view of the mountain beyond. We cut steps to the top of this, from where we could see the next couple of thousand feet. We were confronted by a wide ice-fall, not particularly steep, but so broken that we were doubtful if we could find a route through it. On the extreme right there was a high ice-ridge, easy and unbroken, which ran down to a point opposite to where we were standing. If we could reach it we could avoid the ice-fall altogether. But to do so we would have to climb a very steep ice-couloir about three hundred feet high. The ice was obviously very hard and it would involve several hours of cutting. Also the couloir sloped up from the edge of a high precipice above the Chattumak Glacier, which bounded the ridge to the south. It would be an unpleasant place to negotiate with loads, and there was not time that evening to prepare the way. So we decided to have a closer look at the ice-fall. We climbed on for about eight hundred feet. The ice-sheet covering the ridge formed, along its northern edge, a hanging glacier above the Yam-bulak Glacier. This presumably accounted for the fact that it was split by an unusually large number of crevasses running both up and down the slope and across it. Though the thin covering of snow was very hard, we had a certain amount of trouble in finding a safe route, for it was difficult to avoid both being on the same crevasse at the same time. This intricate structure was reflected in the ice-fall above, which made it remarkably complicated. However, it was wide enough to offer a considerable choice of routes, and although we still could not be certain of finding a way through, we returned to camp having decided to take the chance. On the way back we found two heads of *ovis poli* embedded in the ice.

We started the next morning at a quarter-past seven. We found a way through the ice-fall without any loss of time, though we had to do a certain amount of step-cutting. Beyond, for the next two hours, the route-finding continued to be fairly difficult, and, though we met with no serious obstacle, it would have been very difficult indeed to find the way back in thick weather. At about half-past eleven we reached a conspicuous hollow which we had seen from below, and beyond which the route was perfectly straightforward. Thus far the snow conditions had been perfect and we had made very good time; so good, indeed, that we decided, there and then, to have only one more camp instead of two as we had originally planned.

Beyond the hollow we ran into soft snow and the going became more laborious. By tradition, Gyalgen was carrying the largest share of the load, while Bill and I took it in turns to kick steps. But Gyalgen showed signs of tiring, and as we now hoped to attempt the summit from the next camp, we lightened his load by dumping some of the surplus food and

TUSHUK TAGH : ENTRANCE TO ONE OF THE SOUTHERN CANYONS

PLATE XLIV

kerosene. At half-past three we decided that we had done enough, and pitched camp. While the evening meal was brewing we reviewed our decision to attempt the summit from there. We estimated our height to be at least 20,500 feet, though we had no means of checking it. This left us with rather less than 4,000 feet to climb, which did not seem excessive, given reasonably good snow conditions. We assumed that the soft snow we had lately encountered was the result of melting; by starting at six o'clock we could count on at least four hours of frozen snow. The climbing was devoid of difficulty and we could surely count on making at least 800 feet an hour. The weather was good, though .it seemed to me that there were cloud signs suggesting a change. I confess that the idea of taking up another camp, with all the toil and paraphernalia involved, seemed like breaking a butterfly on a wheel. Bill agreed, though, I think, with less conviction. We settled down fairly comfortably to the long frozen night.

We started brewing tea long before dawn on 13th August. Bill had a bad headache and was obviously not feeling well. Five a.m. is not a good time for making decisions; morally, as well as physically, human beings are at their lowest ebb. It is clear now that we should have reversed our decision of the day before, spent a comparatively easy day taking our camp higher and giving Bill time to recover. Certainly I did suggest it, but probably without enough force, and Bill, being Bill, was not going to agree to it lightly. He had had a headache the morning before, which had disappeared, as such headaches often do, when we had emerged from the stuffy tent. I thought the same might happen again. Whether Bill thought so too, I do not know.

It was beginning to get light by half-past five. We were off by a quarter-past six. The snow was excellent and we climbed a good thousand feet in the first hour. Then things began to go wrong. The snow suddenly deteriorated. It had a thin crust on top which would not hold our full weight but which demanded a sharp kick to penetrate, while in the soft snow below we sank more than a foot; quite one of the most laborious kinds of snow in which to make a trail. This by itself, although disappointing, was not a serious factor, nor was it wholly unexpected. At extreme altitudes there is so little melting during the day that the surface snow does not readily consolidate. In the Everest district, for example, we had found that the monsoon deposits always remained soft above an altitude of 23,000 feet. Two attempts I have made to climb the North Peak have been frustrated by this factor. Muztagh Ata is ten degrees north of Everest, and it seemed reasonable to expect similar conditions at a much lower altitude, though our experience of the day before had been reassuring. However, we could go on for at least eight hours more before turning back, and, unless the snow became very much worse, it seemed inconceivable that we could not climb the remaining three thousand feet in that time. The serious trouble was that Bill's condition did not improve. He could follow in the tracks, but could not lead.

The weather was very clear, but there was a strong wind blowing from the south across the ridge. At first it did not seem to be very fierce or unusually cold, but it must have been peculiarly penetrating, for whenever I paused for a rest I started to shiver as violently as if I had been standing naked in a wind after a cold plunge. Admittedly I had no wind-proof trousers, but I was wearing thick, long, Shetland pants, and four sweaters, while the skirt of my wind-proof smock came down almost to my knees. Gyalgen was the only one of us who kept tolerably warm; he was wearing one of the padded suits worn by the Kashgar Turkis in winter. Bill and I later agreed that we had never been so cold before while actually climbing. The sun reached us at about eight o'clock, but it seemed to give no warmth, either then or at noon. Though the ridge was several hundred yards wide, it was now smooth and the surface of the snow provided no irregularity behind which we could shelter. We could not stop for a moment to rest, so we plugged on, as much in a race to get warm as to make height.

The next misfortune occurred when it transpired, at about nine o'clock, that Gyalgen also was not feeling well and declined my invitation to take a turn at flogging the trail. Why, at that point, we did not turn back, I find it difficult to explain. It was certainly entirely my fault and I can only summon the lame excuse of cold-befuddled wits to mitigate my stupidity. I think my reasoning, such as it was, was something like this : that it was now too late to return, collect the spare food and kerosene which we had dumped the previous day and then to move our camp higher that day; that as, apart from the cold, I was feeling very well, it was a pity not to use at least the morning by stamping a trail which we could follow with much less effort the next day; that soon we would be warmed by the sun and would be able to sit down and contemplate the situation; and, finally, that the good weather would not hold. This line of thought later changed imperceptibly into the feeling, shared more whole-heartedly by my companions, that we must be getting so close to the summit that we might as well go on and finish the job.

I can recall nothing of the next three or four hours except dull, plodding monotony and intense cold. We were prevented by the width of the ridge from seeing the other peaks of the massif by which we might have been able to gauge our upward progress. We avoided going to the left for fear of getting too close to the edge of the ice-cliff overhanging the Yam-bulak Glacier, while to the right the ground was somewhat crevassed. The snow neither improved nor deteriorated; the force of the wind neither increased nor slackened; the sun seemed to become no warmer. Early in the afternoon a small, swiftly moving cloud attached itself to the ridge a few hundred feet above us. This seemed to show that we were getting very close to the top, and I now had very little doubt that we would reach it.

By about half-past two we had reached a point where the slope eased off into what was obviously the summit dome. We reckoned that we must be at least 24,000 feet high, for, apart from the change in the slope, we had now been climbing steadily for more than eight hours, the first of which had been at a very good pace. This estimate was, I think, confirmed by the views of the mountain we had later from the north. But having seen the peak only from the west, we had no idea of the extent of the summit plateau. It was now a question of distance rather than height, and we were depressed by the thought that we might have to go trudging on for hours before finding the highest point in this wide expanse of snow. And yet we might find ourselves suddenly upon it. We decided to give it another hour. But at half-past three we were still not on the highest point, though we can have been only a very few feet below it. With a mixture of relief and bitter reluctance, we agreed to abandon the struggle.

When we started down, I realized for the first time that I was very tired indeed. I had once or twice to call on the others to halt, and once I vomited. But we reached camp in such good time that one more regret, that we had not persisted for just half an hour longer, was added to our contrition. When I removed my boots I found that the toes of my left foot were very obviously frost-bitten. This was most unexpected, for although I had been so cold all day I had not noticeably suffered from cold feet, and I had imagined that I could feel my toes by moving them about in the boots. The boots were old; they had let in the water the day before, and that morning I had noticed that the insides were coated with a layer of ice. But I had put on three dry pairs of thick camel-hair socks. Before this unpleasant discovery, we had been discussing carrying our camp up a couple of thousand feet higher the next day, and from there paying a more leisurely and decisive visit to the summit dome. But my frost-bitten foot put this idea out of count.

We waited for the sun to reach us before starting down the next morning. We stopped to make a brew of jam soup at the site of our first camp, and reached the foot of the ridge in the middle of the afternoon. We could not face humping the loads across to Yam-bulak, so we dumped them under a rock and went on, with the object of sending ponies back for them. But we saw a flock of sheep grazing near by and Gyalgen thought it prudent to stay to guard the loads until the ponies arrived. He did not get in until after dark and was so exhausted that he could not even drink a cup of tea.

The condition of my foot precluded the possibility of attempting to climb Chakragil. Bill might have tried it with Gyalgen, but, typically, he was more concerned that I should get back to Kashgar as soon as possible to have my foot treated. Both he and Gyalgen had had their toes touched by frost, and Bill had at least one sleepless night as a result; but, beyond a blackening of the tips of the toes, they suffered no lasting effects. Our Kirghiz hosts insisted on wrapping my foot in a poultice of cheese mixed with ash from their yak-dung fire. This is the universally accepted remedy for frostbite in these parts. Unfortunately, I cannot testify as to its effectiveness, for, being a man of little faith, I abandoned it after the first day in favour of Sulphonamide.

We went down to the main valley and rested for a day at Subashi, a large Kirghiz settlement, consisting of scores of *akois*. "*Akoi*" is the Turki word (it means literally "white house") for the dome-shaped tent used by all the nomads of Turkestan and Mongolia. (I have not seen it in Southern Tibet.) It consists of a light, skeleton frame of wood, covered with a jacket of felt. *Akois* vary a good deal in size and appearance, according to the prosperity of the owners. Normally they have a floor diameter of about fifteen feet and are about nine feet high. The richer ones are decorated with gaily embroidered felts. The fire is laid on the centre of the floor, and there is a hole in the apex of the tent through which the smoke (most of it) escapes. In heavy rain or snow the hole can be covered by a sheath of felt operated from the outside; then, of course, most of the smoke remains inside. Piles of rugs are stacked all round the walls. A small portion of the *akoi* is screened off for the domestic activities of the women. The inmates sit cross-legged round the fire, and sleep with their feet towards the centre and their heads towards the circumference like the spokes of a wheel. A medium-sized *akoi* can accommodate a dozen people. It is a very comfortable form of dwelling; there is no draught and even in the coldest weather it is kept pleasantly warm inside. It can be assembled or taken down in about an hour and can be carried by one camel or two ponies.

At Subashi we stayed with the Beg (or head-man) in his luxurious and very ornate *akoi*. We spent the day talking to our host and an endless stream of visitors who crowded into the tent, and consumed great quantities of milk and cream. Dinner, which was shared by all who could squeeze into the tent, consisted mainly of great chunks of mutton which were boiled in a vast cauldron and handed round on large steaming platters. There was also a kind of pastry cake, made of flour and cream, which took two hours to prepare; it was delicious, but very rich.

The Kirghiz have a Mongolian appearance, in contrast to the Aryan features of the Turkis. When one has their confidence, they are a most friendly and hospitable people. They lead a free and varied life, moving with their great herds of sheep, goats, yaks and camels from pasture to pasture (usually within the same valley basin), according to the seasons. They make occasional journeys to the oases of the plains to trade their sheep, skins and butter for flour, salt and other needs. Like all nomads of Central Asia, they are splendid horsemen, for, of course, riding is an indispensable part of their lives. Their mode of living precludes real squalor, while their work is free from much of the drudgery of agricultural toil. There is, I suppose, a tendency to over-idyllize the simple life; but if contentment, physical well-

being and a means of livelihood which tends to promote individual dignity and self-reliance together constitute a yard-
stick by which to measure standards of living, then, certainly, that of the Kirghiz is high in relation to the majority
of human beings.

Early the next morning we rode swiftly down the wide,
grassy valley to the Kara Kul, seven miles away, where we
spent another idle day. We chose a flat promontory on the
western shore of the lake and settled down to enjoy one of
the finest views in Central Asia. It was a clear, still day, and
the glassy surface of the lake, four or five square miles in
extent, was very blue. We were at the centre of a complete
semicircle of ice-mountains with a radius of about twenty
miles. To the north and north-east there was an uninterrupted view of the Kungur massif, with its two 25,000-foot
peaks, so laden with ice that throughout its length there was
hardly any rock to be seen. To the east there was a long line
of peaks of the Shiwakte group. The huge mass of Muztagh
Ata filled the southern arc; from here, at last, it showed us a
form and character consistent with its size. Wide grassy
valleys, intersected by rounded hills, filled in the middle distance. Flights of geese and duck passed over the lake. In the
late afternoon we rode over to the northern lake of Basik-
Kul, set in a deep hollow in red and yellow hills and fringed
with meadowland of vivid green. We returned to camp in
time to watch the sunset colours kindle upon the great cirque
of ice-peaks.

The next day we marched on to the north down the Kara-
tash Jilga. Immediately after leaving the region of the lakes,
the valley becomes barren and forbidding, in sharp contrast
to the soft, undulating country that we had been travelling
through almost all the way from Tashkurghan. Bursting its
way over the wide barrier of ancient moraine deposits, which
mark the former extension of the great ice-sheet covering
Kungur, the river plunges down into a conglomerate ravine.
The flooded river forced us to follow a route high up on the

west side of the valley, and we did not reach Bulun-Kul, where there was a Chinese military post, until late in the evening. The commander of the small garrison had died that day. A week before, the bolt of his rifle had burst back into his face while he was shooting *ovis poli,* and had penetrated his skull. My wife, who had spent much of her time while we were on Muztagh Ata ministering to sick Kirghiz who came to her from far and wide, had received a deputation from the garrison asking for medicine for the unfortunate man. Misunderstanding what was said, and in any case quite unequipped to deal with such an emergency, especially at a distance of thirty miles from the patient, she had sent a piece of Elastoplast and some Dettol. This had been accepted by the emissaries with full confidence in an immediate cure.

The lake of Bulun-Kul has almost completely disappeared and its bed is now covered with grass. Immediately north there is a large sandy plain, six miles long and a mile and a half wide, marking the site of another recent lake. This had obviously been formed by the damming back of the waters of the pre-existing Gez and Kara-tash Rivers by the comparatively recent rise of the Chakragil-Kungur massif about them. The resulting formation of the remarkable Gez defile is similar to that of the Arun and other Himalayan gorges. If the modern theory regarding the recent rise of the Himalayas be accepted, cannot the rise of the Kashgar Range (Chakragil, Kungur, Muztagh Ata) also be explained as the readjustment of isostatic equilibrium resulting from the erosion of the Pamir plateau? The drying up of the lake seems to indicate that the cutting action of the combined rivers is now at least keeping pace with the rise of the mountains. It has also resulted in a remarkable feature of the landscape. The country around the entrance of the Gez Defile is subjected to exceptionally violent windstorms, which seem to blow up the defile itself. Since the drying of the lake-bed enormous quantities of sand have been blown from it up on to the hills which flank it on the west, completely filling all the nullahs and forming immense dunes which bury the hill-sides for a thousand feet above the floor of the valley. The dunes look remarkably like the undulating and broken snow-slopes on, say, the northern side of Mont Blanc. It would be interesting to know when these dunes began to form. I can find no reference to them by Hedin or Stein, who visited the area in 1894 and 1900 respectively (I have no access to the account of Stein's later journey), and I cannot believe that they could have been passed unnoticed. Moreover, the 1925 edition of the Survey of India map No. 42 N. which was compiled in this area from Stein's survey, marks the lake-bed in question as a swamp; it also shows the area of the Bulun-Kul Lake as about two square miles, while, as I have said, this lake has now almost entirely disappeared.

We were prevented by the volume of water in the river from travelling down through the Gez Defile, which would have taken us back to Kashgar by way of Tashmalik in four days. Instead, we had to make a long detour to the northwest so as to cross the Kashgar Range by way of the Ulughart Pass. From Bulun-Kul we followed the Gez River upstream for two days, along the southern flanks of the Range. Chakragil was beautifully clear, and we saw that there was a possible route to the summit from this side. It was extremely galling to have to pass it by, and once more I experienced an agony of regret for my stupidity and my carelessness in getting my foot frost-bitten. The valley was wide and green, and interspersed with lakes and swamps inhabited at this time of year by a great number and variety of wild fowl which had migrated from the plains in the spring. It was well populated, too, by large Kirghiz settlements, and we made frequent halts during the day's march to refresh ourselves with milk and curds. Bill aptly described our progress as "*akoi* crawling."

Since leaving Tashkurghan, except for two riding-ponies that we had brought from Kashgar, we had been getting the transport we needed as we went along; an arrangement to be avoided if possible. At Kunti-imes, which we reached on 19th August, our Kirghiz hosts were most reluctant to provide us with the animals we needed to cross the Ulugh-art Pass, which is 16,600 feet high, and difficult for pack-animals. At length, however, after a great deal of argument they produced five ponies and two donkeys (travelling officially, one was compelled to carry a disgusting amount of baggage), with three boys to tend them, none of whom, it transpired later, had been over the Pass before. We were assured that, although the way was long and hard, the Pass could be crossed in a single day from Kunti-imes. In attempting to do this, we let ourselves in for a great deal of trouble.

We started early on the 20th, and were by no means indolent. Throughout the morning we climbed steeply, and by noon we reached the crest of a preliminary pass. From here we had a fine view of Mount Stalin (known to our fathers as Mount Kaufmann), the highest peak of the Trans Alai, a hundred miles away to the north-west. Descending from this first pass, we made our way up a long, desolate, stony valley, adorned with several side-glaciers, until we reached the snout of a big ice-stream coming down from the main watershed. The path then wound its way high up along the steep mountain-side above the glacier, making long detours into deep, precipitous nullahs, cut by glacier torrents. Some of these were very difficult to cross, as they were now dangerously swollen by the melting ice under the afternoon sun. Although the Ulugh-art Pass could be seen from a long way off, these detours made it impossible to tell how long it would take to reach it. Nor, of course, could we get any help from the three boys. Had we known it would take us so long, we would have camped on some flat ground before reaching the glacier, and crossed the Pass the following day. Once we had climbed up on to the steep slopes above the glacier, there was no place on which to make a reasonably comfortable camp; so we pressed on in the hope of getting across before dark.

But it was seven o'clock before we reached the foot of the final slope leading to the Pass. The caravan had straggled badly and some of the animals were a long way behind. The leading ponies were still some four hundred feet below the Pass when the light began to fade. The slope was very steep and the exhausted creatures were making painfully slow progress. It became obvious that it would be quite dark before they could all reach the top; and we had no idea what the other side was like. There was nothing for it but to return to the foot of the slope and spend the night in a makeshift camp beside the glacier.

The night was fine, fortunately, but very cold. The next morning my pony died before he had gone, unloaded, a couple of hundred feet up the slope. He was a large strong animal and had given no sign of undue fatigue the day before, but he had been bred in the plains and was not used to high altitudes. This disaster had a bad effect on the morale of the Kirghiz, who declared that their five ponies would also die before reaching the Pass. They insisted on sending them back with one of the youths, leaving us to transport our baggage as best we could with the two donkeys and what man-power we could muster; for our own second pony was now so weak that it could carry nothing. The entire day was spent relaying the loads across the Pass, a laborious operation in which I could take no active part. The next day we managed to make another five miles down the valley on the other side of the watershed.

A mile or so up a side-valley from this point there was a small Kirghiz settlement marked on Stein's map with the discouraging name of Yamen (Bad) Serai. We sent Gyalgen to lay our sad case before the inhabitants and to try to hire from them four yaks to take us to Yolchi Moinak at the northern foot of the range. This was evidently a tactical mistake; it would probably have been better if my wife had gone with him to inspire confidence. For, though he was unarmed and alone, the Kirghiz mistook Gyalgen for an official come to commandeer some of their flocks. Before this dread invader the male population fled into the mountains, taking with them the faster animals and leaving the women and children and the sheep to his mercy. Gyalgen followed them for a weary day and at length managed to persuade them of his innocent intentions. Even so, he could not induce any of them to come with us; instead, they handed over a herd of a dozen yaks, including three calves, telling him that he might take them to Yolchi Moinak and leave them with the Kirghiz there. Normally the yak is a fairly docile creature, but these seemed to resent being ordered about by strangers. It was only after a prolonged struggle and many abortive attempts that we succeeded in loading our belongings on to the backs of the four least pugnacious beasts and set off slowly down the valley. Gyalgen had had a good deal of experience of the art of yak-driving, and we reached Yolchi Moinak without further misadventure. Here we managed to hire two camels to take us across the thirty miles of waterless desert between the foot-hills and the Opal oasis, where, once more in a land of plenty, our troubles were at an end.

CHAPTER VIII

UCH TASH

I

ACCESS to the high mountains was restricted to a very few months in the year. But the lower mountains to the north, which were accessible for very much longer, provided an unlimited field for travel and minor exploration. Unfortunately, any journey in that direction meant approaching the Soviet frontier and, although they never said as much, the local authorities were not very happy about our going there lest we should run into any trouble. I had assiduously cultivated a reputation for being a keen huntsman, which provided a plausible reason for our otherwise inexplicable passion for travelling in these wild places. However, I generally considered it best to say nothing about our trips in this direction so as to absolve the authorities of responsibility which would otherwise have impelled them to provide us with an armed guard, always a tiresome burden both to us and the Kirghiz with whom we used to stay. But this policy had the great drawback that we were liable to run into trouble with small frontier posts that we went near. It was essential to have with us a Kirghiz from the district, who could establish friendly contact with the nomad tribes and explain our identity. Once, my failure to take this precaution led to infinite trouble.

On our frequent week-end trips to the mountains north of Kashgar, we established close friendship with a delightful family of Kirghiz at a tiny mountain hamlet called Suget. Whenever we went there, we were welcomed as members of the family. The son of the house, Mohammed Khurban, was a very skilful and enthusiastic hunter, and our week-ends there usually had as their main objective the stalking of ibex

and ram chikor, which was an interesting occupation in itself
and provided us with long and glorious days in those remote
and very lovely hills. With the ibex we usually succeeded;
with the ram chikor we nearly always failed. But I had an
ulterior motive with Khurban, which was to entice him to
come with us on our journeys. He was quite willing, when
we promised him some hunting. Gyalgen was oddly jealous
of Khurban, who, of course, was in far better physical condition for moving about the hills, and he protested that the
Kirghiz would be useless to us when we took him out of his
district.

To the north-west of the Min Yol Range there was a large
triangle of country which, so far as I know, was unexplored
by Western travellers. It was bounded on the north-west by
the Soviet frontier and comprised nearly a hundred miles of
the extreme western end of the Tien Shan. The mountains,
which were not glaciated, did not appear to exceed seventeen
thousand feet in height, and I supposed that it would be
possible to travel through the area in the spring. From Ulug
Chat, a village about one hundred and twenty miles west of
Kashgar along the Irkestam road, there was a wide valley,
known as Uch Tash, running up in a north-easterly direction
into the heart of the mountains. It was so large that it seemed
probable that its basin must drain a considerable proportion
of the area. In the early spring of 1948, shortly before my
wife left Kashgar to return to England, she and I, Doctor
Allan Mersh, Gyalgen and Khurban made an attempt to
explore this valley. On 27th February we sent our ponies,
unloaded, to a place called Uksalur, eighty miles along the
Irkestam road, which was as far as we could take our Ford
lorry, in which we followed ourselves a couple of days later.
From here we hoped to travel due north and cross a range
of mountains into the Uch Tash Valley. In this way we
hoped, first, to cut short the journey to the Uch Tash Valley
by two or three days and, secondly, to avoid contact with the
police-post at Ulug Chat. We then proposed to travel to the

head of the Uch Tash Valley, where we hoped to find a pass leading eastward to the country to the south of the frontier pass of Turugart, which we had visited the previous year, and so back to Kashgar.

At Uksalur, a grazing-ground inhabited by semi-nomadic Kirghiz, we were told that, although there was a pass across the range to the north, it was quite impassable at this time of year, as the snow was still lying shoulder-deep upon the mountains. I found this hard to believe, as the country to the north appeared completely arid and not a vestige of snow was to be seen on the southern flanks of the range. However, the Kirghiz were so emphatic, that we decided to change our plan and go on to Ulug Chat, which we reached at noon on 5th March after two days' march. Fortunately, the commander of the police-post, a Turki, turned out to be an old friend of ours to whom we had once given a twenty-five-mile lift into Kashgar. After a little persuasion, he agreed to allow us to travel up the Uch Tash Valley. He told us, however, that we would not be able to get far, as the upper part of the valley was still blocked by great masses of snow and ice. He urged us to come back in June, when, he said, the upper valley was very beautiful, miles of meadows waist-deep in flowers, and enormous herds of ibex and *ovis poli* grazing on the high mountain pastures.

We marched for two days up the Uch Tash. In the first part, the floor of the valley was composed of wide stretches of grassland, over which the river meandered through a chain of deep, clear pools. A dozen miles up, we reached a zone of dense jungle, interspersed with patches of swamp which were inhabited by a large number and variety of water-fowl. At first, villages were fairly frequent; higher up, these gave place to collections of *akois* situated farther and farther apart. Eventually, after we had passed through a great limestone gorge, at about forty miles from the entrance of the valley we reached an encampment known as Karakchi, set at the junction of many valleys. We were told by the inhabitants that at this time of year there was no habitation farther up the valleys. Certainly the country was beginning to look rather bleak and cold, though so far there was no sign of the great masses of snow we had been led to expect. However, we decided to stay for two days at Karakchi and explore the surrounding country. The Kirghiz told us that there was a route up one of the valleys running to the south-east, which led over the high range to the south to a place called Karanglik on the Irkestam road some thirty-six miles west of Kashgar. There was another up one of the valleys to the east, which led over a pass at its head to Toyan, a grazing-ground to the south of the Turugart Pass. In normal conditions both Karanglik and Toyan were three days' march away, but both routes were now quite impassable.

On the first day, while my wife was enjoying a rest after the strenuous marching we had done, Mersh, Khurban and I, with one of the local Kirghiz, rode some distance up the valley to the south-east. Before we had gone more than half a dozen miles, there was a remarkably sudden change in conditions. The flanks of the valley were covered to a great depth in snow, while the bed was overlaid with hard, slippery ice. Travelling in these northern ranges in the summer, we had encountered frequent heavy rainstorms. Now we had further evidence of the extraordinary difference in the climate of these mountains from that of the waterless desert flanking the Tarim Basin, not thirty miles to the south. On both sides of the valley we saw hundreds of both ibex and *ovis poli,* the largest herds of these creatures that I have ever seen. The former were all on the northern flank of the valley and the latter on the southern.

As we went, the valley became steadily narrower, and with every mile the depth of the snow on its sides increased. After a while the icy bed over which we had been riding became covered with soft snow, which was soon so deep that it was impossible for the ponies to go any farther. We had been approaching a massif of fine limestone peaks which were by

INSIDE AN AKOI

KIRGHIZ WOMAN

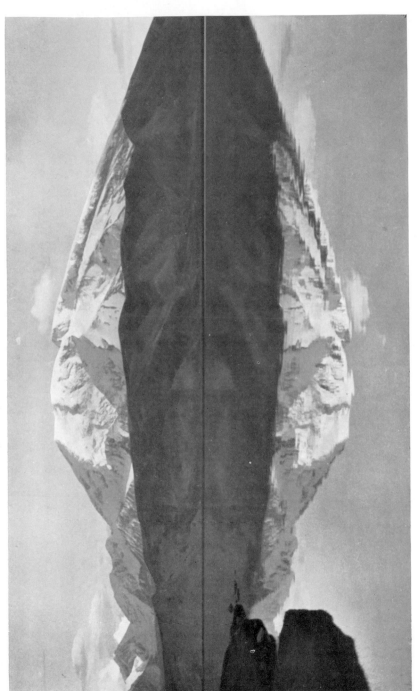

KARAKOL AND MUZTAGH ATA

far the highest in the district, and which I supposed must lie on the axis of the range forming the southern watershed of the Uch Tash valley system.

By now, Khurban, who had also been sceptical, and I were quite convinced that the upper valleys in this region were inaccessible at this time of year. We turned back and retraced our steps for about a mile down the valley. Then, leaving the ponies tethered, we set off up a nullah in the northern flank of the valley in search of ibex. I would have preferred to go after the *poli,* but the snow on the southern flank was far deeper than on the northern. As it was, the going was extremely hard work and after a while the Doctor decided to remain below with the ponies. I asked him to take them to the foot of the next side-nullah, down where we expected to find the game. But we soon spotted a herd in the upper part of the nullah we were in. It was a difficult business to approach them. Providing we kept to the crest of ridges, the snow was relatively shallow, but as soon as we left them to find cover, we were floundering up to our waists. However, after a two-hour stalk I managed to shoot an ibex with a very fine head. While the two Kirghiz were carrying it down, I went ahead down to the main valley to bring the ponies back. Two hundred yards below the foot of the nullah I came upon saddlery and bits of harness scattered over the snow, which was stained with blood. Half a mile farther on I found the Doctor leading one of the ponies, trying to approach a second, while a third, a mare, stripped of harness and saddlery, was floundering in the snow a little way up the side of the valley. The fourth had bolted down the valley and was nowhere to be seen. Apparently, soon after the Doctor had started to lead them down the valley, a fight had started over the mare, and the resulting stampede had been quite impossible for one man to control. Poor Mersh had been trying to retrieve the situation ever since. Between us we managed to capture the three ponies we could see and to recover most of the jettisoned harness. By the time we returned to the foot of the nullah, the Kirghiz had arrived with the dead ibex. It was already past six o'clock and less than an hour's daylight remained. Leaving one pony with them, the Doctor and I rode off down the valley as fast as the slippery surface would allow. It was almost dark before we caught up with the missing pony. Its passions cooled, we had no difficulty in catching it. We tethered it to a rock, where it could not be missed, and rode on in the gathering darkness, which, but for the starlight and the whiteness of the snow, soon became complete. The route, which had been easy enough in daylight with a guide to lead us, was now anything but straightforward. In several places it led along narrow snow-covered ledges on the side of the valley to avoid some impassable defile or cliff. But I soon discovered that my pony, which I had brought from Kashgar, apparently remembered every step of the way. Several times, when I thought that we had gone wrong and I tried to coax him on to another line, he refused to budge until I abandoned the struggle and gave him his head; then he went on with perfect confidence. It was ten o'clock before we reached the cluster of *akois* at Karakchi. We sent two men back to help the Kirghiz, who arrived with their precious burden of meat an hour later.

The next day, while the Doctor went shooting chikor in the vicinity of the camp, Khurban and I, with another of the local Kirghiz, rode up the valley running to the east. For the second day in succession, it was beautifully fine; these were the only two fine days we had during the whole journey. The valley was more open than the one we had followed the previous day and the sides less steep. The early sun sparkled on the ice-fringed river and upon the billowy surface of snow which stretched away on either hand. It would have been perfect country for skis. After riding for about three hours, at a point where the river disappeared under a great depth of snow, we tethered the ponies and began to climb the northern flank of the valley. Although it was laborious work, by following a gentle ridge we managed to keep in snow which was no more than knee-deep, and in another three hours we reached a little peak on the crest overlooking the next valley to the north. It was a splendid view-point and we sat there for a long time while the Kirghiz explained the local topography, pointing out the routes to the passes leading over to Toyan and Karakchi and to another which led across the Soviet frontier. From here the whole range appeared as a vast, wavy sea of snow, and, except for the knot of limestone peaks to the south, I could distinguish no familiar object.

While we were sitting there, I was astonished to hear the familiar call of ram chikor, and soon we saw a dozen of them half a mile along the ridge to the west. It was difficult to imagine what could have brought them so far up into that barren waste of snow; so far as I could see, there was not a scrap of grazing for many miles around. Khurban at once seized the shot-gun, which he had insisted on bringing as well as the rifle, and set off in pursuit, while I sat lazily watching his stalk, which, though skilfully executed, ended as usual in the birds flying off just before he could get within range. On the way back Khurban and I between us shot three ibex, which provided a very acceptable gift to our hosts in Karakchi.

We had, of course, to resign ourselves to returning to Kashgar by the way we had come. The weather deteriorated the very next day, but, except for an occasional flurry, the snow held off until after we had reached the end of the Uch Tash Valley. Nearly all the way from Ulug Chat to Uksalur it snowed gently, though it was not heavy enough to obscure the track or to cause us any serious inconvenience. But on the night we reached Uksalur, 12th March, it snowed very heavily. On the morning of the 13th, a dense mist enveloped the country, and although it had stopped snowing, we found that a foot of new snow covered the ground. None of the local Kirghiz was willing to come with us to show us the way. They assured us, with the bland confidence of all country people who have known their surroundings all their lives, that even in these conditions we could not fail to find our way. We did not share their confidence, but we were reluctant to wait, for we had already been away longer than we had intended and there was no means of telling how long these conditions would persist, even if no more snow fell.

We started at eight o'clock. As we had expected, the route was extremely difficult to find. It crossed an interminable series of steep-sided nullahs, each closely resembling the last. Sometimes it would go straight across; sometimes it would follow the nullah for a long way up or down to reach an accessible exit. Although our helpless flounderings in deep drifts between boulders made it quickly obvious when we had missed the route, it was always surprisingly difficult to find it again, and having found it to divine its direction. We all went on foot so as to stamp a trail for the ponies, and by exercising extreme care we maintained contact with the path for three hours. But somewhere around eleven o'clock we went seriously astray. We spread out and cast about in every direction without finding the elusive path. Although by now the mists had lifted and visibility had been thus extended to about half a mile, none of us could recognize a single object in the landscape. The whole aspect of the country was, of course, totally different under this deep covering of snow; also it was far too broken and difficult for us to march on a compass bearing. Even the physical labour of searching for the path was most exhausting, and it would have been impossible for the ponies to go far without it. At length, soon after noon, we had to admit that we were lost. I was just formulating a somewhat desperate plan of trying to make our way down the nullah to the valley of the Kizil Su, where perhaps there was less snow, as an alternative to following our tracks back to Uksalur, when two horsemen emerged from the mist and rode across the nullah three hundred yards below. We shouted to them, but they would not stop. However, they were going in the right direction and all we had to do was to follow their tracks. By six o'clock that evening we had reached ground so much lower that much of it was already uncovered and the route was clearly visible. That night we found shelter in a deserted hut by a stream. By making two more very long marches, we reached Kashgar on the 15th March.

II

Two months later I had an opportunity of making another visit to the basin of the Uch Tash. I only had ten days at my disposal, but I hoped that by travelling fast and carrying our small requirements in saddle-bags instead of on pack-ponies we would have ample time to reach Karakchi from the east, thus establishing the link across the ranges from that direction. I was very anxious, among other things, to see the wonderful flower-covered alps that the local Kirghiz, as well as the policeman at Ulug Chat, had described. It was still rather early in the year, but in Kashgar it was already full summer and I supposed that something of spring must by now have come to these comparatively low ranges. In any case, it was the last chance I was likely to get. I had discussed with Khurban a probable line of approach to the Uch Tash Valley, westward from his home at Suget. He was familiar with the first two marches and with the local Begs in the district.

I sent a tough young Turki, who went by the pet name of Kapak, and who often came with us on our journeys, to Suget to warn Khurban of our coming. Gyalgen and I followed a few days later on 12th May. I was dismayed to find that Khurban was away from home, having gone off, shortly before Kapak had arrived, on some business of his own. This was a disaster, for not only had I been relying on him to show me the first part of this hypothetical route, but, vastly more important, to introduce me and explain my innocent purpose to the tribesmen we met. And there was no other able-bodied young man in this tiny hamlet to take his place. Khurban's relatives were very upset at my disappointment and suggested sending an ancient uncle to help us on our way. But, after some discussion, the latter wisely thought better of the offer. I thought seriously of abandoning the expedition, but the temptation was too strong and I decided to go on alone with Gyalgen and Kapak, and hope for the best.

A strong north-westerly wind blew during the night and by morning the thick dust haze that had hung over the country for the past two weeks had cleared away. When we set out at seven o'clock, the air was beautifully clear and the outlines of the distant mountains were sharply defined. It was a most remarkable landscape, even in this country of strange forms and colours, and it never failed to fascinate me, whether it was half-hidden by the misty gloom of the dust haze, or dark and forbidding under lowering storm-cloud, or, as on this morning, clear and vast, lit by the soft light of the early sun. The wide horizon was formed by a sinuous ring of mountains enclosing what must in recent geological times have formed a great gulf of the inland sea. Its floor, broken by steep rocky "islands" and now scored into a labyrinth of ridges and canyons, which exposed the horizontal bedding planes, was for the most part grey, but splashed here and there with great sweeps of vivid colour. Our way led close by a curious outcrop of volcanic hills, which from a distance looked remarkably like a line of crimson sponge-cakes, over which black chocolate sauce had been carelessly poured. To our left was the range of mountains which we had so often explored in search of game.

We crossed this range by a deep gap known as the Bai Kurut Dawan, and descended to the great gorge of the Chakmak River, which had its origin on the main divide of the Tien Shan, near the Turugart Dawan. At the little village of Bai Kurut at the foot of the pass, we met a young man who had once received treatment at our Consulate dispensary. He insisted on entertaining us to a meal in his *akoi*. It was now eleven o'clock, and having had no breakfast that morning we were not reluctant to accept. From Bai Kurut I had hoped to travel due west out of the Chakmak Valley and across a pass direct to the next major valley in that direction. I had seen the lower part of the river draining this valley. Khurban had referred to it as the Uruk, and had told me that it flowed from the north-west. We had agreed that its head must lie very close to the Uch Tash, and that from there it would be an easy matter to find a pass leading over to the latter. But our host and his friends assured me that there was no way of getting out of the Chakmak Gorge immediately to the west, and that the quickest way of getting to the Uruk Valley was to go up the river until we came to the first tributary on the left. I was reluctant to go far in that direction, for two reasons. First, the farther north we went, the longer and more complicated the crossing between the two valleys would become. Secondly, about seventeen miles up the gorge was the Chinese post of Chakmak Karaul. Travelling in that district the previous summer, my wife and I had become embroiled with the commander of this post, fortunately on our way back, and although he had been perfectly friendly, I realized that if he came to know of my presence his hospitality would severely restrict my travels. However, there seemed to be nothing for it and we went off up the gorge.

We had ridden for about ten miles, crossing and recrossing the turbulent river as it swung from side to side of the gorge, before we reached a prominent side-valley coming in from the west. It had been an exasperating and rather profitless day; but now at last, at five o'clock, we entered new country and my spirits rose. It was a delightful grassy valley, in pleasant contrast to the grim gorge we had just left. But my enjoyment of the country and the soft evening light was short-lived. The wind had been blowing strongly throughout the afternoon, and before we had gone more than a couple of miles up the new valley it increased to a gale. Clouds of fine sand came sweeping down the valley and struck against our faces with stinging force, and for short periods blotted out visibility so completely that we had to stop until the gust subsided. Farther on we passed some Kirghiz settlements, where we found that the people had removed the felt coverings from their *akois* to decrease the wind-resistance and prevent them from being blown away. They sat with their backs to the wind hanging on to the frames and patiently waiting for the gale to subside. At about seven o'clock we reached a fork in the valley. On a wide stretch of grassland between the two rivers there was a substantial stone building, and in this, with considerable relief, we took refuge from the storm.

The place belonged to the local Beg. He welcomed us warmly, and did not seem for a moment to question our identity. He gave us a room to sleep in and soon produced a steaming meal of "sucash." Moreover, he was most encouraging about the route. He told us that we could reach Uch Tash in two days; the first across a high pass called the Kara Bel Dawan to the Uruk Jilga, the second, over an easy saddle at its head. He agreed to send a man with us across the Kara Bel to a place called Assan Tolmak, where another man would escort us onwards. All this sounded very satisfactory and I went to sleep with a feeling of peace and pleasurable anticipation. This was heightened the next morning when, soon after dawn, we started up the left-hand fork of the valley. The morning was fine and still. The valley was flanked by smoothly curved grass slopes, topped by fine limestone crags, from which the enchanting call of ram chikor floated down on the cool sunlit air. We saw a herd of ibex on a crag high above us, standing motionless against the sky. The valley was short and at its head we could see the pass, a U-shaped gap between steep rock walls. Only one disquieting thought disturbed this delightful prospect. Our

long northerly trek up the Chakmak River had taken us uncomfortably close to Chakmak Karaul. It seemed to me very
probable that the commander of the post would get wind of
us, and send some men to bring us back, if only to explain
ourselves and our movements. At best this would cause a
delay of two days, which I could not spare. So throughout
the morning, while we plodded slowly up the long steep
slopes towards the pass, I kept glancing apprehensively back
down the valley, expecting to see a couple of galloping
horsemen approaching. I felt quite illogically relieved
when we reached the pass and began to descend the other
side.

The view beyond the pass revealed an intricate complex
of steep, narrow valleys all draining towards the south.
Three miles down we reached Assan Tolmak, which consisted of a single *akoi*. The owner emerged from it, looking
scared, but when he had received an explanation from our
guide and a number of small presents from us, his expression
lightened. We were ushered into the tent and plied with
curds and cream, while our host bubbled over with geniality.
He said he would gladly send his son with us to show us the
way. He agreed that we could easily reach Uch Tash the
following day if we started at once; first, we must go a short
way down to the main Uruk Jilga, then follow it up-stream
to its head, whence a gentle pass would lead us to our goal.
No mention was made of any difficulties such as snow-
blocked valleys, lack of grazing or any other of the obstacles
of which we were soon to hear so much.

Paying off our first guide, we went on down the valley. Its
general direction was somewhat east of south and it was far
longer than I had expected. When we had covered another
seven miles, I estimated that we had reached a point opposite, and only a short distance across the mountains from,
Bai Kurut in the Chakmak Valley. Our new guide agreed
that we could have crossed over from there in a few hours.
Our detour had cost us a long day's superfluous travel. When

at last we reached the Uruk Jilga, he announced that he would come no farther as there were no settlements up the valley and therefore nowhere for him to spend the night. I was convinced that this was untrue, but he was adamant. We could probably have forced him to come on, with the threat of a complaint to the Beg. But we had hitherto been received with such friendliness that I thought we could dispense with his services, which were valuable, not so much as a guide, but as a guarantor of our goodwill. In this I made a fatal mistake, which soon became apparent.

It was obvious from the size of the river that we had a very long way to go before reaching the head of the Uruk Jilga. But the general direction of the valley, slightly north of west, was satisfactory, for if this were maintained, I reckoned it must lead us to the country in the vicinity of Karakchi. Before we had gone more than a couple of miles, we met a party of Kirghiz evidently returning from a hunting expedition, for they had portions of ibex carcass slung across their saddles. They seemed oddly scared of us, and when we explained who we were they obviously did not believe us. They assured us that the route up the valley led nowhere and that there were no further settlements in that direction. They were clearly determined to be as unhelpful as possible, so we bade them good-bye and continued on our way. Whereupon they rode after us and said that one of their number would come with us to the next village, blandly ignoring their recent denial of its existence. Their purpose was evidently to keep an eye on us, but we thanked them for their kindness and started once more with our new companion.

All this gave me an unpleasant foreboding of trouble to come. But it was a glorious evening, and the valley was very beautiful. It was wide and grassy; great peaks and ridges stood above it, made of a limestone so white that the snow, which lay deep in the upper corries, was almost indistinguishable from the rock. So, cantering over the soft green turf towards the declining sun, I forgot all else in the exquisite loveliness of the place. Whatever the outcome of our journey, whether we reached our goal or not, the experience of this moment was reward enough.

At about half-past seven we reached a group of four *akois* where we stopped for the night. Though convention demanded that we should be invited indoors, our reception was chilly. The atmosphere was warmed somewhat by a generous gift of rice, soap and tea, but this did not establish our identity, which was obviously suspect. Nor did our liberality win us the slightest encouragement: the pass over to Uch Tash (whose existence was, however, admitted) was many days' journey beyond the farthest settlement in the valley; the country was bleak and desolate, without water or grazing or fuel; up there we would find the snow waist-deep; and even if we succeeded in forcing our way over to Uch Tash, which was highly improbable, we would find it uninhabited and would die from want and exposure. The most that we could achieve was a promise that one of our hosts would come with us to the farthest settlement in the valley.

We started at half-past six the next morning. In a narrow defile a couple of miles on, we saw a herd of ibex on the crags some two hundred feet above the river. Our new companion showed considerable excitement, which I found encouraging, for hitherto he and his friends had been careful to display nothing but polite scorn. Hoping to complete the breakdown of this icy barrier with a supply of meat and the promise of more to come, and to gain favour and prestige which would certainly be transmitted to our future contacts, I dismounted and took aim at a large buck that stood gazing down on us. But I had carelessly neglected to clean the bolt of my rifle after the dust storm of two days before; it was choked with grit and clicked ineffectively as I pressed the trigger. I tried again without success, and by the time I had taken out the bolt and cleaned it the whole herd had disappeared. It may well be that this incident sealed the fate of our expedition;

for by it we lost face we could ill afford and which we had no chance to recover.

Beyond the defile we passed an old fort with a rampart built across the valley. The general direction of the latter changed to north-north-west, which was less satisfactory from our point of view. The limestone gave place to shale and slate, and in consequence the mountains were less attractive. At frequent intervals we passed small settlements of two or three *akois,* each with large flocks of sheep grazing on the ample pasturage. We met several travellers coming down the valley; from each we asked for information about the route. Some said it was four days' journey to the head of the valley, others said two; some said they knew nothing about it, others declared that no route existed.

At half-past eleven we reached a village, which our guide assured us was the last. We stopped to enlist help, and, as was the local custom, we entered one of the *akois,* sat down and made ourselves at home. The whole male population of the village followed suit and the usual tedious conference began: Who were we? Where were we going and why? But English Consuls don't come into the mountains for *tamasha* (the word is used in Turkestan for all forms of frivolity, from a theatrical performance to a short country walk). "On the contrary, all Englishmen like to go to the mountains for *tamasha.*" This was obviously not believed. As usual, I tried to interest them in a free supply of meat. They admitted that there were large herds of ibex and *poli* up the valley. "Why not come with me, then? I have come mainly for shooting and have plenty of ammunition, but I do not want the meat." This was a tactical error and drew the obvious retort, "Why, then, do you want to shoot?" "I want to get the horns." "But we can give you as many as you like." To explain that it did not count unless I had shot the animal myself was obviously useless, particularly as it was a matter about which I was myself far from clear. I abandoned the struggle. My main objection to going on alone, apart from the valuable time we would lose by searching for the right pass, was the fact that, with the valley leading in its present northerly direction, there was danger of our straying across the frontier, which would almost certainly have disastrous consequences. However, we could at least go to the head of the valley and see how the land lay.

"Well, come or not as you like," I told them. "We are going over to Uch Tash to shoot *keek* (ibex). We would be grateful if you would tell us about the route." They replied that it was impossible to go farther up the valley; the snow was waist-deep and even if we survived, our ponies would certainly perish. Thus we talked in circles for about two hours. We were about to take our leave and move on when a large cavalcade arrived, headed by the Beg of the upper Uruk, and including, I noticed, most of the men we had met and questioned that morning. Courtesy demanded that we should stay and explain ourselves to the Beg, and the tedious conversation was repeated. As politely as possible I signified my disappointment at the unhelpful reception we had met with. Whereupon the Beg said that if we would come with him to his place a short way down the valley, he would show us an easy way from there to Karak-chi; it was only two days' journey and he would either come with us himself or send a man as guide. I was far from sure that he meant what he said, but I could hardly refuse his offer after all that talk, and we set off down the valley again at a steady canter, accompanied by the Beg and a large retinue. On and on we rode, into the evening, until at length we reached a place near the fort, only a few miles from our starting-point that morning. We crowded into the Beg's *akoi*, and a meal was prepared by his women-folk from rice provided by us and meat by our host. After which I retired to my little mountain-tent, with the assurance that all would be ready for an early start the next morning.

I woke at dawn to find that an inch of snow had fallen. As I expected, the Beg and his companions used this circumstance as an excuse for going back on his promise. I pointed out that the day was very fine and that at this time of year all the new snow would be gone in a couple of hours. They retorted that though there was little in the valley, higher up in the mountains we would find that it had fallen to a depth of several feet. This was obviously untrue, and after some argument I ordered my horses to be saddled, informed our hosts that we would revert to our original plan, bade them a somewhat curt good-bye and rode off up the valley once more. Soon, however, they overtook us, full of apologies and assurances that their promises would be implemented. By now I had abandoned hope of reaching Uch Tash; a journey in any direction from here would be interesting; so I decided to yield with good grace.

A surly, sour-faced individual was appointed our guide. It was difficult to make him speak, and nothing would induce him to smile. He led us up a small steep nullah to a low gap in the mountains to the west. From here we had a sweeping view westward over a wide, open valley system to a cluster of fine peaks very much higher than the rest of the mountains in the district. I was fairly sure that it was the same massif that we had seen to the south of Karakchi whose whereabouts relative to our surroundings I could now visualize with reasonable clarity for the first time since we had left Suget. It was closer than I had expected and my hopes of reaching it began to revive. The air was still beautifully clear and the sun shone dazzlingly on the new snow. But a mass of black cloud was developing in the south-west, which threatened bad weather.

We rode down the other side of the gap and soon reached the floor of a valley as wide, and containing a river almost as large, as the Uruk. At the point where we reached it, there were two *akois*. Our guide handed us over to the owner, who readily agreed to take his place. We rode on up the valley in a north-westerly direction and in an hour and a half reached another group of *akois* where we halted for a meal. Here, for the first time for several days, we received a really friendly welcome and, what was more, ungrudging information about the route. If the snow conditions on the pass were good, we were told, it was possible to reach Karakchi in a single day from there. But it was a difficult pass and so dangerous in bad weather that many Kirghiz had lost their lives on it. No one had crossed it that year, so they did not know what the snow was like, but if the weather held we could probably manage it. The most encouraging thing was that our new escort resolutely declined to hand over his charge to our hosts, declaring that he knew the way well and would get us across the pass if it were possible. I could have hugged him.

We started again at one o'clock. The weather was beginning to look decidedly threatening and a cold, blustering wind blew in our faces. In spite of this, I felt more cheerful and more able to lose myself in the interest of my surroundings than I had for days. The mountains looked bleak and unfriendly, and there was a considerable depth of snow lying on the slopes, particularly the north-facing slopes, a couple of thousand feet above us. But the valley itself was attractive; there were frequent green meadows and great quantities of juniper which offered the prospect of a pleasant camp and good grazing for the ponies. Some of the juniper bushes were like small fir trees. I was surprised to find such luxuriant growth of this plant, for in the neighbouring valleys it had been sparse or non-existent. We saw several large herds of ibex, but no *poli*.

By five o'clock it began to look as though we had reached the upper limit of the juniper, and when we came to a small grassy side-nullah, well protected from the wind and watered by a clear stream, I decided to camp. A fire was quickly lit and water set to boil, and while Kapak and the Kirghiz remained behind to deal with the ponies and pitch camp, Gyalgen and I went up the nullah to collect juniper fuel. I took my rifle in case I should get a shot at an ibex, for we had been over-generous in distributing our food, and our supplies were beginning to run low. We went about half a mile, round a right-angled bend in the nullah, and so were out of sight of the camp. We climbed a little way up the hillside and worked for about half an hour. Then we started back, each with a large load of firewood.

Suddenly we saw five mounted men, obviously Chinese soldiers, riding up the nullah towards us. My heart sank. As they approached, they deployed so as to surround us. One man dismounted and aimed his rifle at us. We tried to appear as unconcerned as possible and walked towards him with our innocent burdens. But our demonstration failed in its effect. Our adversary, now twenty yards away, was extremely excited and made it quite clear that he would shoot if we did not alter our policy. I flung down my load and put up my hands in the approved style. But Gyalgen was evidently ignorant of this convention, and continued, under his massive stack of juniper, to shout plaintively, "Englis, Englis." I roared at him to follow my example, but he either did not hear, or thought he knew better how to deal with Chinese soldiery. For one horrible moment I expected to see him shot. He was a few yards ahead of me and I ran to overtake him. This diverted the attention of the soldier to me (a result I had by no means intended) and he swung his rifle in my direction. Then I remembered that I had my rifle slung across my back, and though this was clearly the best place for it from the point of view of the soldier, it occurred to me that its presence might be causing him offence. On the other hand, it also occurred to me that if I started to remove it he might regard this as an act of aggression. However, the *status quo* was obviously unsatisfactory, so, as casually as possible, I turned my back on him, unslung the offending piece and dropped it, with profound relief, upon the ground. This had the desired effect. The soldier lowered his rifle and stopped shouting his threats.

By this time the rest of the troop had closed in, and a

very young officer appeared on the scene. My explanation of my identity was obviously not believed. We were searched; the innocent contents of my pockets (glare glasses, a pipe, etc.) were removed and we were escorted back to the camp. Here I was amused to find the Beg of the Uruk Valley and three of his friends, including our sour-faced guide of that morning. They looked rather sheepish and ignored my friendly greeting. I was now able to produce my passport and a Chinese visiting-card. The young officer examined these, blushed and said, "I am velly solly," which I soon found was the extent of his knowledge of English. Tea was ready, cigarettes were passed round and we sat down to a friendly chat.

It transpired that the post at Chakmak had, after all, got wind of our suspicious presence in the neighbourhood, and had sent word of it to the officer in charge of the district at Kizil Oi, on the Irkestam road, fifty miles west of Kashgar. The Beg of the Uruk Valley had also sent a messenger, travelling day and night to Kizil Oi, reporting our whereabouts. It was now clear that his main purpose had been to delay us as much as possible; in this, his admirable balance of diplomacy and obstruction had succeeded pretty effectively. It was interesting that our repeated assertions that I was the British Consul-General from Kashgar on pleasure bent were so completely disbelieved that it had not even been mentioned as a possibility in the reports that got through. These had stated categorically that we were Russians. The Kirghiz whom we had met had not, of course, been able to read my papers. On receipt of definite information as to our whereabouts from the Beg, the Commander at Kizil Oi had sent out a "flying squad" to capture us. None of them had been in that district before, but the Beg and his friends had followed us over from the Uruk Valley so as to meet and guide them and to be in at the kill. The whole operation had been carried out most efficiently, and showed remarkable co-operation between the Chinese Army and the Kirghiz

nomads of the district. The young lieutenant later claimed
that he and his men had travelled 300 li (100 miles) that day.
Though that was an over-estimate, they had certainly done
well. He was most courteous and friendly, and showed not
the slightest annoyance at the trouble I had caused.

I was so relieved by the peaceful outcome of the encounter, whose ugly possibilities I had perhaps been inclined
to exaggerate ten minutes before, that I almost forgot my
disappointment at this obvious frustration of my plans. The
lieutenant had been sent from Kizil Oi to capture me, and it
was clear that, even now that he knew who I was, he could
not allow me to go on without orders from his commanding
officer. We avoided the subject for some time, and then I
suggested that I should remain where I was for the night so
as to go shooting the next morning, for I hoped at least to
visit the pass. But even this he was reluctant to permit, and
I was clearly not in a position to press my request. Though
it was getting very late, Chinese manners forbade any hurry-
ing over these negotiations. For my part, I continued to
nurse the forlorn hope that the lateness of the hour might
induce the lieutenant to relent and allow me to stay where I
was for the night. It was a quarter-past seven before we had
packed up our kit and started down the valley towards the
small Kirghiz settlement where we had exchanged guides
that morning and where the soldiers had dumped their food
and other belongings on their way up.

It was an exhilarating ride. The dark storm-clouds, which
still hung above, had wide rifts in the west which allowed
the rays of the setting sun to strike up beneath them, casting
a weird reflected light upon the vivid green of the valley and
the grim mountains above it. The air was fresh and invigorating. For an hour, before it became too dark, we raced
one another at a breakneck speed, which seemed to me quite
crazy considering the roughness of the ground, and which
the soldiers' ponies maintained with remarkable vigour after
their very long day. After dark it rained. I amused myself by

riding ahead to watch again the sureness with which my pony picked out the route. A young moon, shining through the cloud, was little help. We reached the *akois* at a quarter-past ten, though Gyalgen and Kapak, who had the bulk of our baggage on their ponies, did not get in until midnight. The women of the *akois* prepared a meal from flour and meat brought by the soldiers. The lieutenant and his men were cheerful and very friendly, but the Beg and his pals, bitterly disappointed, I fancy, by the turn of events, were silent and rather morose.

The following day we made a long march down the valley and reached Kizil Oi in the evening. I found that I had met the colonel in charge of the post before; he greeted me with great cordiality. Later, he administered a gentle and well-deserved rebuke for my having wandered off towards the frontier without having notified him; but he brushed aside my apology by making it appear that he was at fault for having spoilt my trip. He insisted on my staying with him for at least two nights so that I could visit some oil-wells that were being worked in the hills to the south. My host slept, ate and worked in a mud-plastered room, furnished with only a wooden table and chair and a rough wooden bed. Another bed was put in for me. The colonel apparently spent his spare time teaching himself English from a couple of very bad phrase books; and on both nights I was there we sat up till after midnight while I went through the books with him. By the end of that time we had practically re-written them.

For the trip to the oil-wells I was provided with an excellent mount with a high cossack saddle, and accompanied by my friend the young lieutenant and two Turki soldiers. As none of them had been there before, we missed the way and spent most of the day riding at great speed through a labyrinth of those fantastic gorges by which most of the desert hills surrounding the Tarim Basin are honeycombed. We reached our objective in the middle of the afternoon, though it turned out, after all, to be only a couple of hours' ride from Kizil Oi. The oil, which was mostly in the form of a solidified pitch, was dug out of deep grottoes in the sides of a nullah. It was carried on donkeys to Kizil Oi, where it was refined in primitive distillers into kerosene, the daily production of which amounted to about five gallons.

We left Kizil Oi at dawn the following day, 19th May. My pony, well fed and refreshed by his rest, was in good form and covered the fifty-odd miles to Kashgar by two o'clock that afternoon. Gyalgen and Kapak followed in a more leisurely fashion and got in twenty-four hours later.

CHAPTER IX

URUMCHI AND THE HEAVENLY
POOL

THE provincial capital, Urumchi, lies about a thousand miles by road to the east-north-east of Kashgar. Until 1935 the only means of communication between the two cities was by cart or by pony or camel caravan. The journey took normally about two months each way. During the last fifteen years a very rough motor-road has gradually been developed, and now quite a number of lorries ply between the two places. Travelling fast one can cover the distance in about a week; Chinese lorries often take as much as a month. However, the bulk of the traffic is by the old method; even the mail still goes by cart, though by a relay system, and travelling continuously day and night, it takes only three weeks.

Throughout my first tour in Kashgar I tried persistently to obtain permission to visit Urumchi, as there were many matters that I wished to discuss with the Provincial Government. I met with equally persistent refusal until, in the summer of 1942, I asked once more to go there to meet my successor, Michael Gillett, who was coming from Central China to relieve me, and to bring him back with me to Kashgar. To my surprise my request was granted. Hitherto, each refusal had been accompanied by the monotonously reiterated excuse that the Tupan was indisposed, and would therefore not be able to receive me in a manner fitting for the representative of a friendly Power. In my ignorance, though partly because I had long grown tired of looking for signs of a change of heart, I at first assumed that this unexpected success was due simply to my new line of approach. But the lengths to which the local authorities went to facilitate my journey, and the unwonted cordiality with which I was received by the officials in the various towns on the way, soon gave me an inkling that there was something more to it than that.

We started on 28th July, travelling in the Ford V-8 30-cwt. lorry which had been brought to Kashgar by Sir Eric Teichman on his journey across Central Asia from Peking in 1935. Gillett was due to reach Urumchi about the end of July; not wishing to keep him waiting, I set out to perform the journey as quickly as possible. At least that was the reason for my haste given to the local authorities, and with which I tried to persuade myself. My real reasons were selfish. I had hitherto regarded a long journey by lorry as the worst form of purgatory to be met with in the more common methods of travel. To my mind there were only two tolerable ways of tackling the ordeal. Either one must grit one's teeth and drive as fast and as far each day as the machine and the human frame would stand, in order to get the business over as soon as possible; or one should loiter sufficiently long at each halt (several days at least) to recover mentally and physically from the racket and discomfort of each stage. In the circumstances the latter method would have taken far too long, so I chose the former. Actually I have always derived very great enjoyment from my journeys to and from Urumchi. The country along the route is so spectacular, so varied and so strange that not even the hideous discomfort of motor-travel could wholly spoil its enchantment. Of course, it was a great help to be in command of the vehicle in which I was travelling; to be able to start punctually at the time planned, to be able to choose the halting-places along the route, and above all to be able to sit for the bulk of the time behind the steering-wheel, the only tolerably comfortable seat on any lorry.

The old caravan road, of course, followed the line of oases fringing the northern edge of the Takla Makan Desert. So does the "motor-road," except for the first two hundred miles where it follows a line some ten miles north of the oases, along the desert close under the foot-hills of the Tien Shan. Actually, in 1942, although the construction of a motor-road had been started in places, it was nowhere possible to use it, and except for this first two-hundred-mile stretch, where the stones had been swept to the side of the way, we followed the country roads of the old caravan route.

We left Kashgar at four a.m. For the first ten miles we drove northward, until we had crossed the gap in the line of desert hills in that direction. Then we turned east, and for the rest of the day we ran across gently sloping desert, close under the steep, barren foot-hills. Sometimes these presented an aspect of towering precipices, vividly coloured by alternating strata of green, red and yellow sandstone. The surface of the track was quite good except for the fact that every two hundred yards or so it was intersected by the deep ditch of a dry water-course. These required very careful negotiating in bottom gear, so that we could never get up any speed. The heat and glare reflected from the desert were unrelenting. We halted an hour for lunch, and for five minutes every hour and a half to fill the radiator. At seven o'clock in the evening, when we had covered 185 miles, we reached a stream containing the first water we had passed for 135 miles. We camped there for the night and started again at dawn.

Immediately after crossing the stream we ran into soft sand, into which the lorry sank to the axles. The only means of progressing was by laying planks for the rear wheels to run over. We had brought these planks against this contingency which occurred many times during the journey. In this way we covered the next three hundred yards in about an hour, after which the surface became fairly firm again. We now joined the line of oases, and followed these, driving along the rough country roads, to Aksu, which we reached at eleven o'clock. I had intended to get to Bai, about a hundred miles farther on, that day; but the authorities in

Aksu had been warned of our coming and they insisted on our staying there for the rest of the day and for the night. We were entertained to a sumptuous feast, and plied with brandy and rice-wine in such quantities that I could scarcely maintain any semblance of dignity, and which gave me cause, the next morning, to regret the otherwise welcome change in the political atmosphere.

Aksu is the largest and most fertile oasis in Southern Sinkiang. There is much greater luxuriance of vegetation than in Kashgar or Yarkand; the willows grow to twice the size; there are wide areas of scrub jungle, inhabited by pheasants; there are extensive swamps, pools and waterways.

We left in the early dawn the next day. We had to wake the night-watchman to open the massive wooden gates of the city to let us out. The road ran north for eight miles to Kona Shahr, the city of tombs. A white mist blanketed the rice-fields, from which the trees loomed in spectral shapes. Night still clung to the loess cliffs which towered above us on our right. Straight ahead, floating above the mists, yet with their capture of the earliest light the only clearly defined objects in view, were the great ice-peaks of the Central Tien Shan. I had not seen them before.

Thirty miles farther on, beyond the oasis of Jam, we entered a broad belt of tamarisk and desert poplar, a veritable forest. I have since travelled through this in the late autumn; it was like passing through a forest of flame, for the desert poplars were then slender cones of untarnished gold, and the tamarisk tumbling fountains of crimson. Beyond, we crossed a wide river, shallow, but unbridged and with a bed of soft, clinging mud. Then followed a forty-five-mile stretch of parched hills, with steep climbs up and down through narrow, twisting canyons and across three passes. At two points along this stretch there were springs of sweet water, where lonely inns catered for the needs of the animal caravans. The track was very rough, which restricted our speed to an average of some ten miles an hour. From the third pass we looked down upon the oasis of Yaka Arik, the first of a continuous string, stretching through the town of Bai, for the next sixty miles.

So it went: stark desert, flat or rugged, alternating with fertile oasis or tamarisk jungle; on the right the grim emptiness of the Takla Makan always near; on the left the Celestial Mountains, and here and there a rare vision of lofty snow-peaks.

We reached Karashahr, some seven hundred miles from Kashgar, on the afternoon of the fifth day. Thus far the towns and villages had been similar to those on the southern side of the Takla Makan, in that their population is mainly Turki. Karashahr, being the centre of the Kalmuk tribes, is predominantly Mongol. The town is built on a swiftly flowing river, as wide as the Rhine at Coblenz, which we crossed by ferry. A few miles farther south, the river flows into the lake of Bagrach Kol, which is fifty miles long by about ten wide. The lake appears to be the breeding-ground of great numbers of ducks and geese. Its exit flows through a narrow gorge by the side of the road in a deep, clear stream which has sufficient volume to carry it across two hundred miles of flat desert to the mysterious Lop Nor.

From Karashahr the road runs for 140 miles up and over a range of barren mountains, a south-easterly offshoot of the Tien Shan, to the rim of that extraordinary basin known as the Turfan Depression, one of the most remarkable geological features in the world. Though it lies in the very centre of the great land-mass of Eurasia, and is thus the farthest point on the earth's surface from the sea, parts of its floor are a thousand feet below sea-level. From the 6,000-foot pass on the southern rim, the road plunged down through a steep gorge. Here we had to work hard with a crowbar to clear a way through masses of rock debris which had fallen from the cliffs and blocked the road at frequent intervals. Since then another route has been found down a gorge with more stable sides. We emerged from the gorge in the

late afternoon onto a wide shelf of desert, formed by
gigantic alluvial fans, sloping down to the floor of the basin.
Below us was an opaque mass of dust, like a cloud-sea but
without its sharp definition of outline. Above this, curving
away to our left and right, the walls of the vast crater were
now clearly defined. Across it, to the north, the glaciers of
Bogdo Ola glistened in the slanting sunlight. Then we ran
down into the dust-fog and the mountains disappeared. We
reached the Toqsun oasis on the floor of the Depression as
night was falling.

In the summer the heat in the Turfan Depression is
terrific. Many of the inhabitants have had cellars constructed
beneath their houses to escape from it. A fierce wind
develops every day about noon as the floor of the Depression
becomes heated. It blows incessantly throughout the afternoon and evening, sweeping up great clouds of dust. Here in
the winter it never freezes; and it is a strange experience to
come from the frigid regions surrounding the basin—from
Tapanchen, for example, a bare fifty miles away, where the
normal winter temperature is far below zero Fahrenheit—to
this warm and sun-baked land. As in the Tarim Basin, it
hardly ever rains. The rivers from the surrounding mountains mostly disappear into the wide desert slopes which
skirt them, so that the inhabitants of the Depression have
to rely largely upon water pumped from wells and labori-
ously constructed subterranean aqueducts.

From Toqsun the road climbs once more to the north,
across sloping desert into stark, arid foot-hills. Crossing
these by way of a steep pass it descends suddenly into an
enchanting valley filled with dense willow jungle, and
watered by a lovely, clear river. This it follows for a dozen
miles, and so across the main divide to the fertile plains of
Tapanchen. Beyond the pass the whole character of the
country changes. The deserts, the arid mountain ranges, the
rich, irrigated oases of South Sinkiang, give place to the
wide steppe-land of Dzungaria or North Sinkiang. The dust

haze, which for eight days out of ten spoils the view in the south, is almost entirely absent in the north, where on most days the clear, often rain-washed air enables one to see for a hundred miles in any direction. With this change of scene there is, too, a great change in the character and culture of the people. Han Chinese and Tungans form a high proportion of the population. Their influence is everywhere to be seen, in the towns and villages and on the farms. The Khasaks, in their colourful robes and headdresses, usually mounted on their stocky steppe ponies, are much more in evidence than are their nomadic counterparts, the Kirghiz, in the south.

We reached Urumchi at noon on the seventh day, thereby, I was told, beating the previous record for the journey by some five days. Word of our approach had been telegraphed from Toqsun, and in a willow grove five miles outside the town we found a large deputation, including Gillett and the heads of the various Provincial Government departments, gathered for my reception. After this ceremony, Gillett and I were driven into the city in the Tupan's limousine. We were comfortably housed in a suite of rooms in the Foreign Affairs Department. There was no British or American Consulate in Urumchi in those days. After two years of isolation from European society, I had an insatiable appetite for talk. The flood now burst on the head of poor Gillett. He bore with me with kindly tolerance, though he had sometimes to drive me from his room in the early hours of the morning in order to get some sleep.

Urumchi is not an attractive place. A bazaar of unspeakable squalor surrounds the walled city. Inside the wall the streets are cleaner, the buildings are fairly well constructed and a number of modern shops lend a superficial air of metropolitan prosperity. But, as is usually the case when a modicum of Western culture is imported to an Eastern town, it has lost all character. Urumchi is treeless; it is begrimed by the soot of the coal which is dug from mines a short way

off; in the winter it is utterly bleak; in the spring the melting
snow turns its streets into quagmires; in the summer dust
and smells predominate. It has, however, one saving grace:
it is easy to get out of the town into most attractive country.
The river-beds are flanked by wide stretches of woodland,
interspersed with occasional lakes and reed-swamps. Most of
the surrounding country consists of undulating downland
covered with coarse grass and small scrub. Once out on this,
either on foot or on horseback, one is soon out of sight of
the drab ugliness of the town. To the south and south-west
the distant view is filled by a fine sweep of mountains forming the eastern ranges of the Tien Shan. Though many of
the peaks are ice-covered they are of no great height; but
their arrangement presents a splendid sense of space and
distance. Their foot-hills, a few hours' journey away, are
covered with thick fir forest. To the east the downs sweep
upwards and soon merge into the great mass of the Bogdo
Ola Range.

Bogdo Ola has the charm of isolation. Though it is really
an easterly extension of the Tien Shan, it is separated by the
deep and wide gap between the Turfan Depression and
Urumchi. The range is ridged by a score of bold granite
peaks arranged in a line from west to east. Two of these are
so much higher and more massive than the rest that from a
distance they completely dominate the scene. Seen together
it is difficult to tell which of the two is the higher. Neither
has been accurately measured, and the various estimates that
have been made of the altitude of the highest point of the
range are wildly divergent. *The Times Atlas* marks it as
22,770 feet. Doctor Grœber, the geologist of Merzbacher's
Tien Shan Expedition, who visited the range in 1903 and
made a rough map of the area, puts the height of the western
mountain at 6,500 metres (21,626 feet). The Survey of India
map, *Highlands of Tibet and Surrounding Regions,* marks
no high peaks in the area. The western mountain is generally
regarded as the highest of the range, though this is probably

due to the fact that from Urumchi it is the dominating feature of the whole landscape, while its rival cannot be seen at all.

Gillett and I had expected to stay in the capital together for about a fortnight, while I completed my business with the Provincial Government. We were well entertained, and provided with a limousine to drive about in; in the afternoons we were taken out to bathe in some hot springs near by; and on most evenings we were taken to see either Chinese opera or a Russian picture at the "Anti-Imperialist Cinema." At the opera one evening an interesting event occurred. A savage warrior on the stage was executing a violent war-dance with a gigantic spear. As he was whirling the weapon above him, the wooden head became detached from the shaft, flew through the air and struck a girl sitting in the front row of the circle full in the face. Blood gushed from the wound and she slumped over the rail. The audience, who had hitherto paid little apparent attention to the performance, were delighted; they roared with laughter and applause, and although the dance continued as though nothing had happened, all eyes were focused upon the unfortunate girl until she was removed.

Despite these diversions we were not anxious to prolong our stay in the capital. But for some reason, which at the time we did not quite appreciate, our hosts were most reluctant to let us go. Gillett had acquainted them with my peculiar taste for mountains, and when we began to show signs of becoming restive they invited us to visit a sacred lake, known as T'ien Shih (Heavenly Pool), high up in one of the northern valleys of the Bogdo Ola Range. We could not return to Kashgar in any case until our hosts were ready for us to go, so we accepted the invitation eagerly. I had not for a moment imagined that I would have either the time or the opportunity to do any mountaineering and, though I had brought Lhakpa with me, I had left ropes, ice-axes and climbing-boots behind in Kashgar. However, the idea of a trek into these little-known mountains was very welcome, even though the official nature of the trip meant that we would be burdened with a large armed escort. Two minor officials of the Foreign Affairs Office were also detailed to accompany us.

The expedition set out in two decrepit lorries bound for Fukang, a small town forty miles along the northern highway from Urumchi to Hami. From Urumchi, Bogdo Ola does not show to advantage. The rounded foot-hills forming the end of the range screen the ice-peaks, and only the very apex of the high western mountain can be seen. But from a point some twenty miles along the Hami road the whole of its great northern flank came into view. With its hanging glaciers and its steep ice-couloirs leading up to the long summit ridge, it was a very impressive sight.

At Fukang we sat for several hours with the magistrate and the local police officer drinking tea and talking polite platitudes while pack-transport and riding-ponies were being arranged. At length, after the usual prolonged argument with the magistrate as to whether or not we should spend the night with him, we set off towards the mountain. We soon reached the foot-hills, made our way up a wooded valley and halted for the night in a pleasant spot. Beyond, the valley narrowed to a gorge. We were told that the lake was only about a dozen miles away but that the gorge was impassable at this time of year owing to the summer floods. The alternative was to make a long detour to the west. We started at six o'clock the next morning, crossed a series of bare, rounded ridges and descended again to another valley, thickly wooded with deciduous trees. A few miles farther up this valley we turned up a steep side nullah to the left and were soon amongst fir forest.

The weather, which had been fine in the morning, turned cloudy and threatening in the afternoon. By evening we were still climbing up through the forest, and the pass by which we were to cross over to the lake was still a long way off.

Gillett and I were in favour of camping in the forest, but our Chinese companions were strongly opposed to this plan, having little faith in the ability of the small mountain tents we had brought with us to protect us from the weather. It was eight o'clock when we reached the pass. Beyond, we looked down over a wide basin flanked on all sides by steep, fir-covered mountains. Heavy rain-clouds overhung the lake, and hid it from view. A short way below the pass there was a wide, grassy shelf, breaking the downward sweep of the forest. On it I was relieved to see three or four *akois*. We were soon sitting comfortably round a fire on rich carpets, drinking large bowls of *kumis* (fermented mare's milk).

The *akois* of the Khasaks are almost identical with those of the Kirghiz, and, of course, their way of life is very similar. I have found that they are a good deal less hospitable and friendly; though, as with the Kirghiz, one's reception varies considerably from place to place, and it is perhaps unfair to judge from my limited experience of the Khasaks. But it is generally accepted that they are more truculent and less amenable to control, and their suspicion of strangers is only to be expected. The Chinese appear to have a considerable respect for them. On this occasion, however, their hospitality left nothing to be desired. The customary sheep was killed in our honour. Usually I struggle hard to avoid this ceremony, and more often than not I succeed. But as guests of the Government we could not protest too loudly. Moreover, our escort had to be fed and they would certainly not have forgone an orgy of meat to which they considered themselves entitled, and which for them was certainly the only mitigating feature of this otherwise intolerable journey.

The next morning we awoke to find everything shrouded in dense mist. I climbed up through the forest and on to the ridge that we had crossed the previous day. I had not gone far before it started to drizzle. After two years in South Sinkiang, where it hardly ever rains, the fresh, damp smell of the forest was sheer delight. Soon I emerged, at the upper limit of the firs, upon steep, grassy slopes. A slender granite pinnacle, cleft from top to bottom, stood upon the crest of the ridge. Rounding this, I disturbed a covey of ram chikor; they plunged, screeching, down into the mist. I sat for a while wrapped in a blanket of silence. From time to time the clouds opened, once revealing, far below, the dark waters of the lake. I returned to the camp, and, about eleven o'clock, we all went on down through the forest. It was raining more heavily, and by the time we reached the lake we were thoroughly wet. A short way above the shore we came to an old Taoist monastery where we secured comfortable lodging.

The next morning was brilliantly fine. Coming out of the monastery, we saw the whole of the lake for the first time. It was about two miles long by a mile wide. The surface of the water was calm and very blue. The eastern shore was overhung by precipitous slopes, dark in the shadow of the rising sun. The western shore, fringed with firs, and the gentler slopes above it were bathed in sunlight. From the farther end of the lake a U-shaped valley ran up towards a curved line of ice-peaks. Of the big mountain, only the ice-dome forming the summit was visible. The scene had all the attributes of the conventional Alpine landscape—the lake, the forested slopes, the ice-peaks at the head of the valley, the dark gorges cutting into the lofty precipices. We might have been a thousand miles, instead of a bare twenty, from the vast, barren steppes of Central Asia. It is a quality peculiar to high mountains, and perhaps one of their chief attractions, this paramount insistence upon the immediate environment, which isolates so completely in space and time and excludes all outside influence.

Gillett and I set off along a rough path by the side of the lake. Winding round innumerable inlets, climbing steeply over rocky headlands, it took us about an hour and a half to reach the farther end. From there we went a few miles up the valley coming down from the peaks. I was very anxious to get a close view of the big mountain. At the time, of course, I did

AKOI

T'IEN SHIH—THE HEAVENLY POOL

not suppose that I would ever have the opportunity of an
attempt to climb it, but the distant views of it from the
Turfan Depression and from the north had been very tan-
talizing. Gillett, too, was keen to prolong our stay in this
delightful country. From the monastery we could see a high
rock pyramid, with a small glacier on its eastern slopes. It
appeared to lie immediately in front of the big mountain,
and to be accessible from a camp in the valley. When we returned to the monastery that evening we announced to the
Chinese officials that we wished to spend two or three days
in the valley beyond the lake. Their faces fell and a prolonged argument ensued. Though, of course, their real
reason for objecting was the fact that they were hating every
moment in this barbarous spot and wished to get back to
Urumchi as soon as possible, they tried to dissuade us by
emphasizing the grave risk we would run of an attack by the
wild and unruly Khasak tribes, and the appalling discom-
forts we would suffer. However, Gillett's command of
Chinese and his powers of persuasion won the day, and they
agreed to allow us to go with a small armed escort.

The next day we went back past the end of the lake and
spent the night at a small Khasak encampment at the foot of
a large tributary valley coming down from the east. At four
o'clock the following morning, an hour before dawn, Gillett,
Lhakpa and I started climbing towards the rock pyramid.
We had considerably under-estimated its height, for, though
we climbed steadily and with little pause, it was half-past
two in the afternoon before we reached the top.

It was a splendid view-point. The morning had been very
fine, but by now clouds had formed. These, however, only
partly hid the ice-peaks and enhanced their height and splen-
dour. The north face of Bogdo itself was revealed as a long
rampart of steep ice-fall and hanging glacier, divided by a
series of rock- and ice-ridges sweeping up to three summits,
evenly spaced on a crest some two miles long. The eastern-
most summit was the highest, and consisted of a magnificent

ice-dome. A large glacier flowed along the foot of the wall.
Throughout the whole length of the face I could see no
practicable line of ascent. On the eastern skyline, however, a
steep rock ridge descended from the ice-dome to a high col
between the main mountain and a small pointed peak. This
col was accessible from the glacier below, and it appeared
that the rock ridge might be climbable. But I remember
thinking that if I ever had the opportunity of attempting to
climb the peak I would certainly explore the southern
approaches before making a serious effort from the north.

We sat for an hour on the summit of the rock pyramid
studying the view, while new aspects of it were constantly
revealed from behind the drifting cloud. We heard the clatter
of stones a short way below us to the west and peeping over
the edge in that direction, we saw a herd of fifteen ibex not
thirty yards away. We must have been sitting very silently,
for they were quite unaware of our presence. The way down
seemed even longer than the way up, and it was dark before
we reached the camp, thoroughly tired after a long and
delightful day.

Our brief visit to Bogdo Ola had been an unexpected and
exciting experience. Having studied only the Survey of India
map I had, stupidly no doubt, hardly suspected the existence
of this range of great ice-peaks, let alone its nature. The very
denial of a close acquaintanceship sharpened my appreciation, though it accentuated in the years that followed the
curious sense of unreality that I feel for all Central Asian
country when I am not there.

It was the middle of September before Gillett and I were
able to leave Urumchi. On the eve of our departure we were
given a farewell banquet, a formidable affair at which some
two hundred people were present. A military band was
stationed at one end of the large banqueting-hall; at the
other end a small round table was set for the guests and the
presiding host. Unfortunately the Tupan himself was "in-

disposed," and his place was taken by Mr. P'eng, his deputy. There were six guests: a visiting Minister of the Central Government, my Soviet colleague and his Vice-Consul, Gillett and myself and my secretary, Mr. Chu. The remainder of the two hundred sat at long tables stretching the length of the room.

There was an order in force at the time forbidding the consumption of alcohol by Government officials. Unfortunately it did not extend to guests; so that whereas at the long tables nothing was drunk but water, at our table the only liquid available was Russian brandy. Each of the chief officials toasted us in turn, and each demanded "Kan Pei" (bottoms up), blandly ignoring the inequality of the contract. In face of such unfair odds, I determined, with unreasonable bravado, to accept each challenge. After the first few toasts, my colleague, who was sitting on my right, and I made a solemn undertaking, in the name of the friendship which would henceforth always bind our two countries, to support each other through the ordeal. But presently I noticed that he was prudently emptying most of the contents of his glass on to the floor prior to each toast, and it seemed clear that he would have to do most of the supporting.

By the fifteenth course I was feeling on top of the world and quite impervious to the effects of alcohol. Indeed, I was looking forward keenly to discharging my part in the evening's entertainment, the thought of which had earlier spoilt my appetite. But at about the time when Mr. P'eng rose to make his speech of welcome, I began to feel very ill. I must have looked at least as bad as I felt, for Mr. P'eng, a kindly gentleman, interrupted his speech to say that if Mr. Shipton wished to go out for a breath of fresh air he was welcome to do so. But with the foolish arrogance common to those in my condition, I rejected his invitation. About this time I noticed that my left-hand neighbour, the minister, had passed out and was lying across the table, peacefully asleep.

Circumstances had placed me in the position of principal

guest, and it was my task to reply to Mr. P'eng's speech. I controlled my nausea with the aid of some more brandy, and Mr. Chu and I rose to our feet. I had planned my speech carefully that afternoon. So far as I remember it was intended to open with some apposite remarks about Central Asia being the cradle of mankind. I plunged straight into my subject and announced: "The dawn of civilization." This profound remark was translated into Chinese by Mr. Chu and thence into Russian by a Russian translator, and I clearly had the engrossed attention of my audience. I repeated with great weight, "The dawn of civilization." Mr. Chu, doubtless taking this for a rhetorical gambit, again translated it into Chinese, whence it was again rendered into Russian. When I repeated the phrase a third time Mr. Chu reminded me that he had already translated it twice. I replied hotly, "Well, say it again." This he did and I sat down amid great applause.

Soon after this we moved to one of the long tables. Here I remember sitting opposite to my colleague, listening with powerful concentration while he lectured me upon the vital importance of co-operation between Britain and Russia. The next thing I remember is walking down the garden path on Mr. P'eng's arm. I am told that I had made a steady passage along the hall and down the great curling stairway, even keeping time to the regimental march which the band had struck up to speed the departing guests, all of whom were in a state as mellow as any host could desire.

In November 1947 my wife and I were in Urumchi and we paid a hurried visit to the Heavenly Pool. This time we were able to go straight up the gorge. The trees were bare and the river small and clear. Large numbers of chikor had come down to the valley to glean the tiny fields and to escape from the autumn snows. Six miles up, the gorge contracted to a steep, narrow canyon, through which the river poured in a booming cataract. The path climbed steeply to a wide, grassy cwm above the canyon. At the far end there was a gentle slope of fir forest, beneath which the river flowed through a subterranean exit from the lake. The winter snows had been late in coming to the plains, but up here it already lay deep in the forest. We reached the shore towards sunset; a pink light was reflected from the mountains beyond on to the surface of the lake. It was very silent. We spent the night in the monastery, and the next day climbed through the snow-laden forest to a rocky crest, two or three thousand feet above the lake.

WHEN Tilman left Kashgar in September 1947 he said that he would like to return the following year if that were possible. During the winter I devised an ambitious programme for the following summer, which not only fascinated me but induced Tilman to overcome considerable difficulties in order to pay me a second visit. My contract expired in July 1948, and as the Kashgar Consulate-General was then to be handed over to the Governments of India and Pakistan, it seemed probable that I would be relieved of my post by mid-August at the latest. I had to go to Urumchi again in June and I suggested that if Tilman could meet me there, having travelled by way of Central China, I could probably spare some time for a trip to Bogdo Ola. After that we would travel back to Kashgar together, possibly visiting the Central Tien Shan on the way. After I had handed over charge of the Consulate in August, I proposed that we should travel to India together by a new route. One of the possibilities I had in mind was a journey involving two hundred miles of continuous glacier travel. Starting from Shimshal in Hunza, we would make our way up the Kunjerab Glacier and over a pass to the "Snow Lake" that Scott Russell and I had discovered in 1939, then over to the Panmah Glacier by a pass that Fountaine and I had found in the same year, then over to the "Old Mustagh" Pass to the Sarpo Laggo and the "New Mustagh" Pass to the Baltoro, up that glacier and across to the Siachen Glacier by a pass yet to be discovered, and finally down that great glacier to Ladakh. The second possibility I had in mind was a journey south from Khotan to investigate a piece of unknown country in the Kuen Lun, south and east of a great

23,800-foot mountain called Muztagh. From there we would travel along the undemarcated border of Tibet and across country recently explored by Colonel Schomberg to Leh. It was certainly an interesting programme, but, in the circumstances, not too ambitious if things had worked out as I had expected. Unfortunately, they did not.

Our meeting in Urumchi was much delayed. Tilman arrived there by lorry from Lanchow on 6th July. Before leaving Kashgar I had received a message from the Govern-

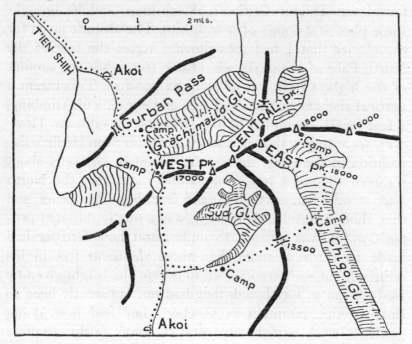

ment of India informing me that my Indian successor would be coming to Urumchi about the end of July, and suggesting that I should wait there for him and drive him back to Kashgar in the Consulate lorry. This poor old machine was by now very decrepit; indeed, it would certainly have been superannuated long ago had it been possible to replace it. I handed it over to the workshops of the Provincial Transport Department in Urumchi to have some major repairs done, and hoped for the best. By the time Tilman arrived I had nothing further to keep me in Urumchi. I had hoped to pay a visit to Ili, but this was politically impossible, and I was free to spend nearly three weeks on Bogdo Ola. While we were in Urumchi we stayed with Mr. and Mrs. Hall Paxton, the U.S. Consul and his wife, whose delightful hospitality my wife and I had enjoyed the previous winter.

Before leaving England, Tilman had searched the library of the Royal Geographical Society for such scant material as existed relating to Bogdo Ola. The most interesting thing he found was Doctor Grœber's sketch-map, and he brought some photostat copies of it with him. The altitude given for the glacier that I had seen flowing across the foot of the North Face of the peaks was 11,000 feet, while the summit of the highest peak was given at 21,300 feet. This meant a vertical rise of ten thousand feet of very difficult climbing, a feat rarely attempted by the strongest expeditions. However, according to the calculations made on Sven Hedin's Expedition in the early 'thirties the mountain was only about eighteen thousand feet. This would mean that the North Face stood a bare seven thousand feet above the glacier, and this, though formidable enough, was a totally different proposition. It was difficult to understand how Grœber had made an error of more than three thousand feet in his estimate, but we were inclined to accept the height given by Hedin's party, for though they had not apparently been so close to the mountain as Grœber, they had been doing geodetic work which necessitated some fairly accurate triangulation.

Tilman and I had been used for so long to conditions in the Himalaya that it was difficult to adjust ourselves to the idea that a mountain of eighteen thousand feet could present a really tough proposition. For there, partly because of the height of the snow-line and partly because of the great elevation of the main mass, peaks of eighteen thousand feet could never be regarded as more than minor heights. Our base camp on Everest had been 16,800 feet, that on Kamet

15,500 feet; the Karakoram Pass was 18,200 feet, and even on Mustagh Ata our first camp had been 17,000 feet high. We had continually to remind ourselves that, though we were still in Central Asia, our latitude (44 degrees) was equal to the southern ranges of the Alps, and a long way north of the Caucasus. Although I had made a study of the mountain from close range, I could form very little idea of its difficulty. All that I could predict with reasonable certainty was that the rock would be good and that the climbing would be of a high order.

I had brought Lhakpa with me from Kashgar. But in the years he had spent there performing his sedentary duties he had grown fat, and it seemed unlikely that he would be much use to us on the higher reaches of the mountain either as a load carrier or as a climber. But, however out of condition, he was always a good man to have on an expedition—keen, intelligent and resourceful. To help us with the carrying of the higher camps I had brought a young Hunza man named Agasha from Misgar, who had a remarkable reputation as a hunter of *ovis poli*. He certainly appeared tough and active enough, and he had never before been anywhere but in rugged mountain country or below an elevation of eight or ten thousand feet. The journey to Urumchi was the first time he had ever been in a motor-car, and when we had started, the staff of the Consulate had pulled his leg mercilessly— telling him that he was expected to ride it like a horse or that it would explode if he rode with his back to the engine. My Chinese secretary aptly named him Hill Billy.

We left Urumchi on 9th July. Bob Dreesen, the American Vice-Consul, accompanied us for the first two days. We took with us enough food for three weeks, some of which I had brought from Kashgar, though the Paxtons, with characteristic generosity, had invited us to take whatever we wanted from their well-stocked store-room. We had my two battered old "Meade" tents, two Primus stoves, two lengths of nylon rope, and a pair each of rubber-soled climbing-boots of Swiss make that Tilman had brought out from home. These were equipped with devices designed for keeping the boots dry in wet snow, one of the most serious problems in climbing at high altitudes. They consisted of skin spats, which were supposed to fit closely over the uppers of the boots. However, we never succeeded in attaching them securely to the boots, and soon abandoned them.

The Mayor of Urumchi had promised me to send instructions in advance to the magistrate of Fukang to arrange for pack-transport to take us up to and beyond the Heavenly Pool. But when we reached Fukang at about eleven o'clock, we found that the magistrate had received no such instructions. However, he was very helpful, and after a good deal of talk it was arranged that we would go on as far as possible in the lorry and that he would collect the pack-animals from the surrounding villages and send them up to us that afternoon. Our anxiety to get out of the bleak, comfortless rooms which characterize Chinese *yamens* and up into the hills was such that, though with some misgivings, we decided to take him at his word. Two local policemen, armed with rifles, were attached to our party. Both were old friends who had come with me the previous autumn and who were apparently so pleased with the tips I had given them that they were keen to come again. They did not realize what was in store for them. We forced the lorry as far as possible, and in the early afternoon settled down in a charming, wooded valley to await, with growing anxiety, the arrival of the pack-transport. When night was falling and we had given up hope, the animals arrived.

The next morning we packed up in the dawn light and were off by six o'clock. We went up the gorge again, and though it was summer we encountered no great difficulty with the river. The air was cool and invigorating. Three hours' steady walking, first through the deciduous woods which filled the lower valley, then through the fir forest, took us to the lake. The sky was clear and the water was still and very blue. We built a fire of pinewood and cooked a breakfast of porridge, fried eggs, toast and tea. Tilman and Dreesen swam in the lake. We basked on the grassy shore until the ponies arrived. There was a large, clumsy rowing-boat which we borrowed and rowed ourselves to the other end of the lake, while the ponies went round by the rocky path. It took us just over an hour, while the ponies took two hours and a half. We went on up the main valley to the place where Gillett and I had camped, and then turned up the large tributary valley to the left. The path followed a steep rocky torrent for two miles and then began to zigzag up the southern flank of the valley through dense fir forest. At about six o'clock we came to a small Khasak encampment just at the upper limit of the trees, and we stopped here for the night. It was a fine position: steep grass slopes behind were crowned by a cirque of crags, from which the long, echoing cries of ram chikor could be heard; in front, the forest plunged down into a deep gorge; beyond, the lower foot-hills melted into a haze which overhung the plains. It seemed incredible that we were only a day and a half's journey from Urumchi and its evil-smelling squalor. The indefatigable Dreesen, determined to make the most of his long week-end, set off in vain pursuit of ram chikor. Bill and I lounged luxuriously by the fire in one of the Khasak tents, drinking tea and smoking until supper was ready. Later that evening the local Khasak Beg turned up, having heard of our arrival. He was a large arrogant man, not particularly friendly. But we had brought a letter of introduction to him from an influential Khasak woman in Urumchi, and he agreed somewhat reluctantly to do what he could to help us.

The next morning Dreesen left very early, as he intended to get back to Urumchi that evening. Bill and I made a late start, accompanied by the Beg and a small retinue of Khasaks. An hour farther up the valley we stopped to collect juniper roots from a patch which the Khasaks told us was the last we should find. A short way beyond, the valley made a right-angled bend to the south. At the corner there was another small Khasak encampment, their highest grazing-ground in this part of the range. The Beg and his friends left us here.

We now found ourselves in bleak, desolate country. Although it was nearly mid-July and though we were at an altitude of no more than ten thousand feet, summer had not yet reached this broad flat-bottomed valley. The ground was still sodden from the newly melted winter snow. Indeed, there were large beds of it still unmelted. The grass and spring flowers had not yet appeared from the muddy soil. The valley was flanked by shapeless rocky peaks, skirted by long scree slopes and smooth, lozenge-shaped glaciers. A cold, blustering wind blew in our faces, and mounting thunder-clouds in the south threatened a storm. The ponies were painfully slow over the swampy ground and the morale of the drivers was evaporating fast. We were making for a rounded saddle at the head of the valley, which we knew from Grœber's sketch-map lay on the main watershed of the range and close to the North Face of Bogdo, which was still hidden from our view. We had planned to put our base camp just on the other side of the saddle. By the time we reached the head of the valley and started up the final slope, it appeared that the storm was just about to break. The slope was gradual but covered with huge boulders, so that the going was very difficult for the ponies. The drivers were most reluctant to go any farther, but somehow we managed to induce them to do so. At last, at about three o'clock, we reached the rounded crest of the saddle. The view on the other side was terrific. A short way beyond, and some three hundred feet below us, there was a wide sweep of glacier. Beyond this, towering up into a dark mass of cloud, stood the huge granite ridges of the mountain, separated from each other by steep ice-couloirs and hanging glaciers. Here and there a window opened in the cloud above, revealing an extension of one of the ridges, and giving an impression of prodigious height and steepness.

Miraculously, the storm still held off. We ran down the slope beyond the saddle until we came to a place that was reasonably level, and set to at once with ice-axes to clear places for the tents. These were ready by the time the ponies arrived. We had just got the tents pitched and most of the baggage stowed away under cover when the storm burst with a deluge of rain. The ponies and their drivers started back at once, together with one of the policemen; the other chose to stay with us, sharing a tent with Lhakpa and Agasha. Lhakpa was feeling far from well. He had suffered from a severe headache during the march, as well as from shortness of breath; now he felt shivery and complained of a pain in the chest as well. It seemed incredible that this veteran Sherpa, however soft he had become, should be suffering from such a bad attack of "altitude" at a mere eleven thousand feet, and though his temperature was normal, we feared that he was sickening for something considerably more serious.

Another cause for concern was the behaviour of the Primus stoves. We could not get them to burn properly. After a struggle we would achieve an even blue flame, and we would settle back with a sigh of relief. But after a minute or so they would begin to gasp like men fighting for breath; then they would burst into flame, filling the tent with black smoke and covering everything with greasy, black soot. Then the laborious process of heating and coaxing would begin all over again. Certainly the stoves were very old and battered; they had been used on Everest in the 'thirties; but Primus stoves do not usually suffer from age, and I have never known mere battering to put them out of action. More likely the cause of the trouble lay in the indigestible quality of the Urumchi kerosene. After two hours of unremitting toil we succeeeded in brewing a potful of lukewarm tea. This was discouraging, for in our higher camps we would be entirely dependent on the Primuses, and, moreover, would have to melt snow for water. Producing water from snow takes at least as long as boiling the water when produced.

In the meantime, the rain had turned to a cold and equally drenching sleet. The tents leaked and our sleeping-bags became wet, while an unaccountable accumulation of mud infiltrated from outside. It was one of those occasions when it seems that the price to be paid in misery and frustration for the doubtful pleasure of climbing mountains is altogether too high. Travel these remote ranges by all means, but confine your camps to the meadows or the forested slopes! Climb peaks perhaps, but go to the Alps for the purpose, where you can enjoy the sound of the weather from the warm security of a hut, and if it is still bad to-morrow, a pleasant swinging walk through mist and dripping pines is all that separates you from a well-cooked meal and mulled wine! The evening closed in on us and it became too dark to read; the holed tent let in too much wind to keep a candle alight. We ate with no relish the cold contents of a tin, and settled down to eleven hours of fitful sleep.

At six o'clock the next morning the wind had dropped. We peeped out of the tent at a cloudless sky. Very little snow had fallen. Agasha managed to get a fire going and we cooked breakfast. This, according to our old custom, consisted of tsampa and well-sugared tea. Tsampa appears to be unknown in these parts of Turkestan, but we had prepared a supply of it before leaving Urumchi. By the time breakfast was over, the sun had reached us and we spread our sodden belongings to dry. Lhakpa was no better; but he was no worse and we decided to keep him with us for another day. At half-past eight we started out, taking Agasha with us.

The geography of this part of the range is remarkable. A well-defined axis of high peaks runs for some ten miles due west from the highest summit. The main mountain (which we had come to refer to as Bogdo) has a crest nearly two miles long on which there are three summits—the highest at the eastern end, the lowest at the western end, though the difference in height between the two is probably not more than a couple of hundred feet. A wide glacier flows westward along the foot of the North Face of this mountain and terminates at the western end of the face. As the eastern and northern boundaries of the glacier are formed by low, scree-covered hills, almost all its ice comes from the steep corries and hanging glaciers of the North Face of Bogdo. The river issuing from the snout of the glacier, instead of flowing down the northern side of the range, turns abruptly to the south and flows clean through the main axis of high peaks through a narrow defile. Another strange feature of the glacier, as we discovered later, is a great tongue of ice near its head, which has broken through the hills to the north. Here, therefore, is an unusual phenomenon of a glacier situated in a normal cirque, yet draining down the two opposite sides of the range. I wished that we had had a competent geologist with us to account for that great defile through which the bulk of the water drained. The idea of headward erosion through those massive granite walls, which formed the peaks of the main axis of the range, was inconceivable; nor could I detect signs of "river capture" on the northern side. It seemed then that here, as is apparently the case with so many formations in the Himalaya, the alignment of the river must have existed before the high peaks.

The going on the glacier was easy; there were very few crevasses and most of the winter snow had gone, leaving a surface of bare, smooth ice. So, as we went, we had plenty of time to study the mountain. The opinion that I had formed several years before about the North Face was confirmed. All the ridges looked terribly difficult, and although on some of them each individual section might have been climbable without loads, they were far too long to tackle without establishing several camps along them, and that would have meant carrying heavy loads up some of the most difficult parts. All the couloirs between the ridges were guarded by hanging glaciers, so that, apart from their steepness and length, it would have been suicidal to attempt to climb them. The only hope of climbing the mountain from this side was the rock ridge which ran down direct from the highest peak in a north-easterly direction to a high col separating the main mountain from a small pointed peak at the head of the glacier. A steep ice-fall led down from the col to the glacier, and though it was very crevassed, it looked as though it would be possible to work up it and to carry a camp to the col. Whatever the height of the col it did not look to be more than two or three thousand feet below the summit. The ridge itself stood out in profile against the sky. It was bisected by a prominent notch, but above and below this it appeared to be set at a uniform angle, so far as we could judge it, of about fifty-five degrees. This is not excessively steep, even if maintained for three thousand feet, provided the rock is good, clear of snow and sufficiently broken.

Our object that day was to make a more detailed study of the North-east Ridge. For this purpose the high col, besides being too far away for our untrained state, would have been too close under the ridge to have provided us with a comprehensive view of it. So we climbed to a lower saddle at the head of the main glacier and to the left of the Small Pointed Peak. From this, we made our way up along a jagged rock ridge to the north-east, away from the mountain until we were high enough to see the North-east Ridge. We were startled by its appearance. It looked far steeper and more forbidding than before. This in itself meant nothing, for it is impossible to judge the angle of a ridge when looking at it end on, as we were now doing. Also the ridge was broad, which would afford sufficient choice of routes. But every ledge and crack on the rocks was laden with a mass of snow, evidently the remains of the winter deposits. We could now see the eastern face of the Small Pointed Peak. Here, too, the rocks were covered with a deep mantle of snow, and though they were nothing like so steep as the North-east

BCGDO OLA : NORTH FACE

BOGDO OLA : EAST RIDGE

Ridge, they would be very hard to climb in these conditions. It was quite clear that it would take many days—even weeks —of hot sun before it would be possible to tackle the North-east Ridge. After this disappointing discovery, we climbed down to the glacier and returned to camp.

That evening it started to snow again, and continued throughout the night and most of the next day; not heavily, but enough to make it impossible to do any useful exploration. During the day the snow turned to rain. Agasha spent a long day hunting ibex, but though he saw a herd in the distance, he could not get close enough for a shot. Bill and I lay in our sleeping-bags discussing plans. We did not agree. Bill thought that as soon as possible we should take a camp up to the High Col and decide definitely whether or not the North-east Ridge was climbable. I considered that before doing anything else we should make a thorough reconnaissance of the mountain. I argued that, with snow conditions as they were, it was un-likely that we could come to any definite conclusion about the North-east Ridge, and that taking a camp to the High Col would therefore be a waste of time; that we might find an easy or, at any rate, an obviously easier route on the southern side; that snow conditions on the southern side would certainly be much better than on the northern; and that even if we failed to find an alternative route, a week or so spent in wide reconnaissance would provide us with much-needed training, and allow time for the melting of the snow on the North-east Ridge, to which we could then return with the stimulating conviction that it was the only route. I sup-pose I argued more forcibly, for Bill, though still not con-vinced, eventually agreed to adopt my plan.

In the middle of the afternoon it stopped raining and we went to examine the route through the Great Defile. We made our way round the snout of the glacier. The river issuing from this was remarkably small considering the great volume of ice that it drained. This was further evidence that the real summer melting had scarcely begun on the north side of the mountain, though the sun was well past the solstice. In the very throat of the Defile we found a big lake. Gigantic granite walls swept up on either side, forming a cup, breached on its farther side by a great cleft which was the narrowest part of the Defile. About two thousand feet above the lake, the walls disappeared into cloud. To the right a hanging glacier loomed out of the mist. Great blocks of ice had recently fallen from this into the lake. As we made our way round the eastern shore, which was composed of vast granite blocks interspersed with grassy meadows, a pair of Brahmini duck flew out from behind a rocky promontory and circled, screeching, above the lake. Beyond the lake the valley plunged steeply down through the Defile and then, a bare mile away, widened out between rounded grassy slopes on the southern side of the range. Though in the gloomy evening light we could not see any sign of habitation, it was clear that we would not have far to go to reach the first Khasak encampments.

In the meantime, Lhakpa was still ill and obviously not improving. We decided that when the pony-men visited us, which we expected them to do with a load of fuel on the following day, we would send him down to the Khasak camp just above the forest, where he would be warmer, more comfortable and supplied with plenty of milk. His illness was our first real misfortune, for though we had not relied on him to take part in the climbing or load-carrying, he was necessary to us as a sheet-anchor for our base camps and for negotiating with the Khasaks, particularly as the morale of the policeman would not stand much more of this bleak and cheerless life. Also, his absence proved a constant source of worry and restricted the range of our travels.

The next day, 14th July, it was fine again. Our first task was to move camp, in several relays, to a large, overhanging boulder a quarter of a mile away, near the lateral moraine of the glacier. Though the boulder gave little shelter to the tents, it provided an excellent kitchen where we could store the wood in a dry place, make a fire and cook, even when it was raining. The move was completed by nine o'clock, and Bill and I set out on our next reconnaissance. The object of this was to cross over to the eastern side of the mountain and to see what lay beyond the North-east Ridge and the High Col. We crossed the col we had reached two days before, descended a glacier on the other side and crossed another ridge coming down from the Small Pointed Peak. We then found ourselves in the eastern cwm of the mountain. It was an impressive affair, formed by the narrow, triangular face of the mountain and bounded on the right by the North-east Ridge, the High Col and the Small Pointed Peak, and on the left by a long ridge running eastward from the summit of the mountain. Before we could get a clear view of the cwm, we had to climb a tangled ice-fall, making our way through a maze of crevasses and ice-cliffs to a flat glacier plateau forming the upper floor of the cwm. From this side the mountain looked tremendously steep and forbidding. The High Col was flanked by some three thousand feet of utterly unclimbable ice and rock. The North-east Ridge itself looked really formidable. The main feature of the face of the mountain was a great ice-couloir of prodigious steepness, topped by what looked like a great overhang. But the East Ridge seemed to offer some hope, if we only could reach it. It was very long; it was obviously narrow and corniced; but its crest, except for its final sweep to the summit, led upwards at a gentle angle. Away to the east it looked accessible from this side, but the approach was up a steep face of ice which was overhung by the great cornices of the ridge. Again I considered that we should explore the southern side of the mountain before committing ourselves to such a venture. This time Bill agreed with me, though he still hankered after a close-up view of the North-east Ridge.

We saw that the East Ridge was a continuation of the

main axis of the range. It formed a high curtain, nowhere less than 15,000 feet, running through several minor peaks and connecting Bogdo with its unnamed eastern rival. We came to refer to the latter as "The Six Thousander," as Grœber had guessed its height as 6,000 metres (19,686 feet). It was a splendid peak.

Having seen all that there was to be seen of the Eastern Cwm, we made our way back down the ice-fall. The journey back to camp was laborious, as the snow on the eastern glaciers had melted in the hot afternoon sun and we sank into it up to our knees.

When we reached camp, we found that the two pony men had arrived with two ponies and a load of wood. Had it not been for Lhakpa, we would have moved down to the gorge through the Defile that evening, and as things turned out it would have been much better if we had done so. But we thought we had better send him back to where we knew he would be comfortable; so he went off, with instructions to send the ponies back as soon as possible on the following day, and also, if possible, to send a yak as well, as we were doubtful if the ponies would be able to negotiate the very rough going through the gorge. Bill set off early in the morning with the object of going as far as possible round the southern side of the mountain so as to look for the best line of approach. I was to await the arrival of the ponies and then bring them and all the baggage through the Defile into the grassy valley beyond, where Bill would meet me. I expected the ponies to arrive by eleven o'clock and I spent a pleasant morning climbing about the hills above the glacier, from which I had superb views of the North Face of the mountain. The ponies did not arrive until three o'clock in the afternoon. I was relieved to see that they were accompanied by a yak. It took me an hour to get the camp packed and loaded on to the animals. I was just about to start when I saw Bill returning up the valley. He had gone without any food, having expected to meet us at about two o'clock. But he was too full of his news, which he recounted as we went, to show any annoyance.

He had descended to the valley below the Defile and had found himself at the junction of a wide tributary valley coming in from the east. Here he met some Khasaks herding large flocks of sheep. They had greeted him very coldly. He went up the tributary valley, which curled round to the north, and he soon found that it had its origin in a great rock cirque which formed the south-west sector of Bogdo. It was bounded on the right by what was evidently the main South Ridge of the mountain. He had a clear view of the ridge, and after careful examination came to the conclusion that there was a perfectly sound route up it. The only question that remained was whether it led up to the main summit ridge and, if so, at which point they joined. From where Bill stood it appeared to culminate in a snow-peak so close to the main summit ridge that it seemed reasonable to suppose that there was a fairly easy link between the two. Also, he was able to identify the Western and Central Peaks of the mountain away to the left, so he assumed that the South Ridge was joined either to the highest eastern summit or to the col between that and the Central Peak. It certainly looked as though he had found the key to climbing the mountain.

As it was still early in the day, Bill climbed, in another two hours, to a col about eleven thousand feet high at the foot of the South Ridge, from which he looked down to a big ice-stream which had its origin in the cwm formed by the south-eastern segment of the mountain. The existence of such a large glacier in this quarter might have warned us that the South Ridge probably did not connect with the eastern summit, but neither of us made this deduction. When Bill returned to the valley junction, he found that the shepherds had been joined by another man who carried a rifle. He was quite obviously hostile. He threatened Bill with his weapon and demanded his coat. However, Bill ignored him and walked on. Some time later, when he had reached the lake, he heard a shout behind him, and, looking round, saw the man two hundred yards behind, aiming his rifle and signalling to him to stop. Again Bill took no notice and the man disappeared.

It was very slow-going with the animals and when we reached the lake we decided to camp on its shore. We chose a delightful spot: a little grassy patch covered with wild flowers, and with a view of the lake between two great granite blocks. Later, the moon came out from behind the eastern portal of the Defile, its light sparkling on the dark waters of the lake and gleaming on the hanging glacier and the steep ice-ridges on the other side of the cirque. Behind us the vast cliffs of Bogdo were jet velvet-black by contrast.

Again it was a slow and laborious business getting the animals down through the rocky Defile the next morning, and it was ten o'clock before we reached the meadows below. The shepherds were there. With the policeman to explain our identity, they were more friendly and undertook to supply us with milk, butter and fuel. They said that they had taken Bill for a Russian, but that they were glad now that they had not shot him. Bill thanked them for this expression of friendship, and after reminding them of their promise of supplies, we went on up the tributary valley and camped just below the point where the pasture gave place to barren scree. We were in full view of the South Ridge and Bill explained the route he had traced on the previous day. It certainly looked quite feasible. From the glacier that filled the upper part of the valley there was a wide snow-couloir running up two or three thousand feet to the crest of the ridge. Near the top of this, we would put our first camp. Then came a section of ridge which was narrow and serrated, but even if we could not climb along its crest, it would not be too difficult to traverse below it. It ended at a buttress three or four hundred feet high, which, though steep, offered a wide choice of routes, both on rock and ice. Above this, an easy snow-slope led to the top of the snow-peak which was the highest point of the South Ridge visible from here. We proposed to put our second and highest camp at the foot of the buttress.

That afternoon I climbed two or three thousand feet up the southern flank of our valley to see the South Ridge in better perspective and if possible to find out what lay beyond the snow-peak. In doing so, I shattered our new-found hopes. Before I had climbed 1,500 feet above the camp the main eastern summit appeared directly behind the snow-peak. There was no mistaking its powerful, thrusting curve, its beautiful, rounded ice-dome. A wisp of cloud in front showed that it was separated from the South Ridge, and as I climbed, it became more and more obvious that a great gulf lay between the two. I saw that the snow-peak in which the South Ridge had appeared to culminate was connected to the Central Peak of Bogdo, but, as we had seen from the north, the ridge connecting the Central with the Eastern Peak was very long and difficult. I had reached a high crest overlooking the next tributary valley to the south, at the bottom of which, on a small glacier, I saw a herd of fifteen ibex. I followed the crest along to the east until it turned into a steep ice-ridge leading to a peak which stood to the south of the col which Bill had visited the day before. Here I found recent tracks of ibex leading up towards the peak.

CHAPTER XI

BOGDO OLA — 2

MY discovery that Bill's route was no good was a great blow. In spite of Lhakpa's absence we were in a good position to attempt it, while to move to another unknown base involved a great many complications. The policeman had already announced his intention of leaving us, and although he could probably have been induced to remain where he was for three or four more days to guard our base while we attempted the South Ridge, he certainly could not have been prevailed upon to go any farther afield. Then there was the question of transport. The pony-men had been extremely reluctant to come so far and we had persuaded them to do so only by promising to pay them off and send them back the next day. The local Khasaks had told us that it was impossible to get animals over the col to the south-eastern side of the mountain and, of course, they would not supply any to attempt what they knew to be impossible. Nor would they agree to act as porters. We could, of course, take a light camp over ourselves, but besides the fact that this would put us in a weak position to attempt any route we might find, we did not trust the local Khasaks to refrain from stealing what we left behind. Once the police-man had gone, we had no means of negotiating with them. Still another point was our reluctance to get too far out of touch with Lhakpa. He had sent a note with the pony-men saying that he was feeling better, but he was still sick. Bill suggested that we might at least attempt the Central Peak by way of his route up the South Ridge. But this would use up so much of our available time and resources that it would put any attempt on the Eastern Peak out of count, and I think we both felt that we would rather fail in an attempt to reach the highest summit than climb the lesser.

However, these problems could be postponed for at least another day. We could explore the south-eastern segment of the mountain from where we were. This would no doubt include the southern side of the great East Ridge which we had seen from the north. If we could prove that there was no feasible route up the mountain from there, the question of moving to a new base would not arise and we would have no choice but to turn our energies and place all our hopes upon the North-east Ridge. So, early the next day (17th), having discharged the pony-men but persuaded the policeman to stay with us a few days longer, we crossed the col at the foot of the South Ridge. We took Agasha with us. It was a laborious climb of about two thousand feet, mostly over scree, to the top, and a delightful run down, also over scree, for two thousand feet on the other side. This took us to the side of a wide glacier which flowed due south between steep rock walls. There was a good deal of cloud about and most of the peaks at the head of the valley were obscured. But we could see what we took to be the lowest part of the East Ridge, a sort of wide col between Bogdo and the "Six Thousander." There was a perfectly straightforward route to its crest.

It looked as though the clouds would lift; so we crossed the glacier, climbed to the top of a rocky knoll on the other side and waited. The cloud lifted slowly and by one o'clock a substantial portion of the East Ridge was clear. It was long and led over a small peak, beyond which it dropped to a col that we could not see. But it looked easy enough to carry loads along. The upper part of the glacier was invisible from where we stood, as there was a sharp left-hand turn in the main valley. Beyond this lay the South-eastern Cwm of the mountain, and from it the glacier issued in the form of an ice-fall, through a narrow defile. In the afternoon we went on up the glacier and eventually succeeded in getting a view

into the South-eastern Cwm. It was in the form of a huge
quadrangle bounded on the left by the South Ridge, which,
at the snow-peak, bent round to the west and connected
direct with the Central Peak of Bogdo; in front, by the long
ridge connecting the Central and Eastern Peaks, and on the
right by the East Ridge. The walls of the cwm were tremendously steep and nowhere less than four or five thousand
feet high. As we turned back down the glacier, the Eastern
Peak came out from the clouds. From where we stood, the
upper part of the East Ridge was very foreshortened and
largely screened by the lower part. But judging by what we
could see and from our memory of what we had seen from
the Eastern Cwm we came to the conclusion that it was well
worth attempting, and anyway more promising than the
North-east Ridge.

Earlier in the day Agasha had complained of a pain in his
stomach. This had got worse and he made very heavy
weather of the climb back up to the col. He refused to eat
anything that evening and the next morning he lay in the
tent groaning. This was another bad set-back. When we
had left Urumchi, three weeks had seemed a generous
allowance of time. We had taken things fairly easily at first,
the best policy while becoming adjusted to the altitude and
mountain exercise. We had not exactly frittered away our
time, yet half was already gone. We could doubtless have
done better by concentrating more determinedly upon a
thorough reconnaissance of the mountain before forming any
conclusions about a route. But, as Bill said, it is so difficult to
make up your mind about a route until you have rubbed your
nose in it. Again, we should have spent at least one of the
next two days in trying to reach the crest of the East Ridge
from our present camp. I think we could have done it in a
very long day, and it would have given us a clearer idea of
what the ridge was really like. Perhaps we had lost some of
the ability for making the right decisions that we had
acquired in our long expeditions before the war. As it was,

we spent two days in useless discussion and negotiation with the Khasaks over the problem of getting our baggage across the col. Certainly we had the excuse that the weather was bad, and a day and a half of light rain damped our zeal for action. We went down to the Khasak encampment in the valley below to try to induce them to take us over to the big glacier by a roundabout route, but we got no satisfactory answer from them. The Beg was away and they could do nothing until he returned. Agasha's illness complicated matters still further, for besides robbing us of his carrying-power, we felt we ought to stay with him in case he took a turn for the worse.

On the afternoon of the 19th, the weather cleared. The sun came out and warmed our spirits, Agasha was a bit better, and although he would not be fit for heavy work for several days, we felt justified in leaving him behind. We had just decided to start relaying loads up to the col, when the Khasak who had been bringing us a daily supply of milk arrived. He had always been more friendly than the rest, and when we told him of our decision he said he would bring his two yaks up the next morning and these would at least carry the loads to the col. That evening, to our great joy, Lhakpa arrived. He seemed to have quite recovered and said he was ready to come with us. Things were looking up.

The next morning the milkman and his two yaks came at nine o'clock and we were off by half-past nine. It was a difficult job getting the yaks up the steep scree, but they managed it and we reached the col by midday. It was not fair to ask our friend to bring the yaks down the other side, as he could not have got them up again alone. But he volunteered to leave them on the col and help us to carry the loads down to the glacier, which we reached by one o'clock. We had lunch, and then the three of us divided up the loads and made our way very slowly up the glacier. Our equipment was by no means light and we were carrying provisions and fuel for a week. The route from the glacier to the lowest part of the East Ridge was up an ice-slope about three thousand feet high, its lower half steep and bare, its upper half comparatively gentle and snow-covered. There was a rock ridge running for about seven hundred feet up the side of the ice-slope. We climbed about three hundred feet up this and pitched our tent, at about six o'clock, on a wide ledge. While I was in the tent getting the Primus going, Bill stood outside looking up at the peak, only the upper part of which was visible, its ridges thrown into sharp relief by the light of the setting sun. Suddenly Bill said: "Eric, we're bats. The upper part of that ridge is bloody awful." But he admitted that perhaps it was not fair to judge from that very foreshortened view. We debated whether or not we should abandon the attempt while we still had time and supplies enough to go back to the north side of the mountain and try the North-east Ridge. But we were both most reluctant to go back now that we had come so far, and we decided to go on and hope for the best: after all, some trick of the evening light might have exaggerated the steepness and narrowness of that upper section of the ridge. Of course, we should have gone up to reconnoitre. We could have gone a long way without loads and, as we found later, we had only to go to the lowest part of the ridge to see all we needed. But the weather was now brilliantly fine and from our previous experience we did not expect it to remain fine very long.

We cooked and ate a huge brew of macaroni and pemmican, and settled down to a comfortable night. We started cooking breakfast before five the next morning, and had packed up the camp and were away by six. We expected to reach the ridge quite easily that day, and our early start was designed so that we should get over at least some of the upper snow-slope while it was still hard. We climbed to the end of the rock ridge and embarked upon the ice. This was rough and we expected to be able to climb it with a minimum of step-cutting. But I think we had under-estimated the steepness of the slope, for with our heavy loads we found it

necessary to cut steps the whole way. It was very laborious
work and our progress was painfully slow. After a couple
of hours, we speeded things up by changing our tactics. The
leader went ahead without a load, cutting tiny nicks in the
ice, until the rope was taut. Then he would cut a large
stance, haul up one of the loads and help the second man to
climb up the nicks by a pull on the rope. Then he went
ahead again while the second brought the third man up. It is
extraordinary how quickly the time passes in such work. At
first, when we were still in the shadow of the East Ridge, it
was painfully cold waiting for the steps to be cut. No
sooner had the sun reached us than we became unpleasantly
hot. I kept trying to estimate the number of rope-lengths
which remained before we reached the easier ground above;
each time that we had completed the estimated number we
seemed to be exactly the same distance from the top of the
steep part of the slope. Lhakpa was not feeling at all well.
Bill and I shared the cutting, but, even so, standing for hours
on a steep ice-slope with a heavy load on your back is a great
deal more exhausting than climbing continuously up-hill.

At about half-past two we reached a point where the slope
began to ease off and we decided to send Lhakpa back.
I lowered him down on the end of our two ropes joined
together, going some way down the slope myself until he
reached easier ground. While we went on working, we
watched him down to the glacier. He would easily cross the
col before nightfall. While we were still on bare ice it was
awkward work dealing with the three loads, as we were constantly in danger of letting one of them slip. Presently, however, we got onto soft snow, into which we sank up to our
hips. Then it was just a question of flogging a track. We
made such slow progress that at four o'clock we gave it up,
dug a platform out of the slope and pitched the tent. We
were still about fifteen hundred feet below the crest of the
ridge. A very hard day's work had brought us about twelve
hundred feet up the slope. We felt tired and frustrated. If

we had made such heavy weather of a comparatively straightforward section of the climb, what hope had we of getting up that long East Ridge with no one to help us with the load-carrying? However, the Primus behaved well, we had found a rivulet of water by digging down to the ice and tea was soon ready. We ate great hunks of bread (which Bill had baked two days before) and jam. Lying snugly in our sleeping-bags sipping mugs of hot, sweet tea, the frustration and fatigue of the day was gradually replaced by a feeling of great contentment. The evening was calm. We could see the whole of the South-eastern Cwm and its immense retaining walls; the sun sank behind the ridge between the Central and the Eastern Peaks, lighting its ice-crest with a nimbus of burning gold; the glacier below was drowned in blue shadow. The snow about us froze, and apart from an occasional sharp report from the ice below, the silence was complete.

We decided the next morning to carry up the loads in relays. We started early, and the snow was frozen so hard that we had to give a sharp kick to obtain purchase on it. In an hour we reached a bergschrund three hundred feet below the crest of the ridge. Emptying our rucksacks there, we glissaded back to fetch the remaining loads, which we carried past the bergschrund and up a steep snow-slope to the ridge. The crest was of ice, narrow and heavily corniced on the northern side. But where we reached it, there was an outcrop of rock.

One glance along the ridge to Bogdo dashed what hopes we might still have nursed of being able to climb it. Although there was a small peak on the ridge between us and the main mountain, there was a slight northerly bend in the ridge which enabled us to see most of its length. The section running over the small peak was very narrow and crowned by a heavy snow cornice the whole way. This would have made it impossible to keep to the crest. The northern flank was composed of ice, impossibly steep. The southern flank was broken by a series of rock buttresses, each one of which would have been difficult to traverse; the prospect of doing so with loads did not appeal to us. On the other side of the small peak there was a fairly deep depression where we had hoped to put our next camp. Beyond this there was an exceedingly steep ridge, perhaps four hundred feet high, which appeared to be composed of hard ice. Beyond this, again, there was another long narrow section, while the final pyramid of the peak looked formidable. We did not have to study it long before coming to the conclusion that it was not for us to attempt to climb the East Ridge.

I have always been of the opinion that the art of mountaineering, in the perhaps limited sense of climbing difficult mountain-sides, can be learnt only in the Alps or some similar comparatively small and much-frequented range. In the first place, in the Alps the length of the climbs are such that they can mostly be done in a day, while huts and other facilities enable a man to spend a very large proportion of his time actually climbing on difficult snow, ice and rock. Given fine weather, there is no reason why, in, say, a month, he should not do some twenty climbs, each twelve or fifteen hours in length, so that at the end of that time he has acquired an immense amount of technical practice and experience. Secondly, the great number of mountaineers who visit the Alps, the fact that a number of experts can, year after year, specialize on one mountain face or on a group of peaks, and also the easy accessibility of the mountains—all these factors have naturally resulted in an exceedingly high standard of performance. And however modest a climber's ambitions, his standards are almost bound to be improved by the raising of the general level: climbs that twenty years ago were tackled only by the most daring experts are to-day undertaken by very mediocre performers. Thirdly, the fact that the climbs are so well known, documented and classified, deprives the mountain of one of its most formidable defences, the unknown; so that, apart from the factors of changing weather and snow conditions, a climber can concentrate almost entirely on the purely technical difficulties. This again, of course, provides him with greatly increased facilities for improving his technique and, even more important, of measuring his skill against an accepted standard of excellence.

In the greater and comparatively unknown ranges, the case is just the reverse. The great distances involved, the long glacier approaches, the slow, laborious business of establishing camps and of reconnoitring, result in only a tiny proportion of the time being spent actually climbing in the Alpine sense. The fact that heavy loads have to be carried a long way up the mountain, the physical disabilities resulting from altitude, the disastrous consequences which threaten from bad weather, these so often make it impossible to accept the challenge of a difficult ridge or face. The emphasis, therefore, is always upon the avoidance of difficulty, and one very rarely allows oneself to be committed to a spell of many hours of really hard climbing, which is a commonplace in an Alpine season. With so many new mountains to tackle, climbs are hardly ever repeated, so that a comparison of standards is almost impossible. Lastly, perhaps the most important element of all, the fact that each upward step is on new ground, each ridge of unmeasured length, each slope of unknown steepness, absorbs so much of the climber's attention and his nerve that he cannot give the whole of himself to grapple with sheer technical difficulty.

Thus a man might spend a lifetime climbing in the Himalaya and never acquire the skill, the experience or the judgment needed to tackle a really difficult mountain (in the Alpine sense of the word "difficult"), which a few good seasons in the Alps would give him. I have always said that if I had to choose, for an Everest Expedition, between a man who had had a thorough training in the Alps and one who had only climbed in the Himalaya, even though his ex-

BOGDO OLA : SNOW-COVERED ROCKS ON
NORTH-EAST RIDGE

BOGDO OLA : CAMP BELOW THE EAST
RIDGE

CHAKRAGIL : NORTH FACE

perience there had been great, I should, other things being
equal of course, unhesitatingly choose the former.

Unfortunately, all skills need practice if they are to be
retained. Just as the athlete will lose his speed, dexterity and
strength without practising his sport, so the Alpine mountaineer may lose, not only his gymnastic agility on difficult
rock, but that instinctive power to distinguish between danger and difficulty, that confident poise on a knife-edged
arête, that acute judgment of difficulties ahead of him, that
automatic adroitness in handling the rope and axe, that
toughness of nerve that can withstand long hours of delicate
movement over, say, precipitous, ice-covered rock, which in
some degree must form part of his stock-in-trade. Thus, as
it is almost impossible to learn the art of mountaineering in
the Himalaya, so, by climbing exclusively in the Himalaya
for a long period, one tends to lose the art one may
have learned. I do not deny that there is a vast amount
that one learns in the Himalaya that one cannot possibly
learn in the Alps, but here I am discussing mountaineering
in the strictly limited Alpine sense of climbing difficult ice,
rock and snow.

In the summer of 1948 it was exactly twenty years since I
had climbed in the Alps. Bill's case was certainly no better.
Tackling the problems with which we were faced in the
mountain ranges of Central Asia, exploring, crossing unknown passes, climbing or attempting to climb great peaks,
we had not been greatly hindered by any deterioration in
our technical ability, though I had always been aware of it
as a fact. Faced with a proposition like Bogdo, it was painfully obvious. Neither of us had tackled so difficult a climb
since we had climbed the West Ridge of Mount Kenya in
1930. Whether, placed in the same position but endowed
with our 1930 form, we would have succeeded in climbing
the East Ridge of Bogdo I cannot say. We would certainly
have tried, and I believe we would have done it. Bill was
inclined to attribute our failure to age; I found our physical

ability to carry loads and to work on the mountain-side sufficient evidence to the contrary.

Even now I suppose we could have turned back and gone
all out for an attempt on the North-east Ridge. It was half-
past ten, 22nd July. We could have got the loads back down
to the glacier before dark, spent the next day relaying them
back across the col and with luck induced our Khasak friend
to lend us his yaks to take a camp back to the north side of
the mountain on the 24th. If the weather held, we might
just have had time and supplies to carry a camp up to the
High Col and to attempt the North-east Ridge. I am not
sorry that we stayed where we were. It was a glorious position on the ridge, and our camp there was one of the best I
have ever experienced.

We fetched the remaining loads from below the bergschrund, dug an ice-platform out of the crest of the ridge up
against the rock outcrop and pitched the tent on it. We
brewed tea from the ice-chips we had cut from the ridge, ate
a large meal and then lay basking in the sun, our legs
dangling over the edge. The view was grand. The western
section was filled with an intricate pattern of superb ice-
ridges and precipices which formed both the Eastern and
South-eastern Cwms, culminating in a slender pyramid of
ice which, as seen from here, was the summit of the highest
peak of Bogdo. Across the Eastern Cwm we could see the
outline of the North-east Ridge, running straight and steep
from the summit down to the High Col. To the south, across
the plain of Tapanchen, were the mountains of the Eastern
Tien Shan. To the north we could see down a wide valley to
the steppes of Dzungaria, featureless as a wide expanse of
ocean. To the east, the ridge, sharp and corniced, swept up
to a snow-peak.

A haze hung over the Turfan Depression to the south-east.
Looking at it reminded me of our remarkable position, sitting up there at 15,000 feet on an icy crest and within sight

of that great hollow in the earth's surface, where the inhabitants must now be sweltering in torrid heat. I wondered if its proximity to the mountain produced any freaks of weather. We were very soon to experience one.

At about half-past four a wind started to blow from the north, and we retired to the tent and started to prepare the evening meal. By half-past five the wind had increased to an extraordinary violence. Looking out of the tent, we saw the sun sinking behind the highest peak of Bogdo. All along the East Ridge a huge wave of ice-particles was breaking over the crest, like spray across a breakwater, lit to a golden brilliance by the sun. Similar waves were sweeping over the Central and Eastern Peaks, forming long, swiftly moving plumes. For a short while the wind became a hurricane, the tent floor heaved under us, and it felt as if we were being swept away. One of the guy-ropes snapped, and one end of the tent collapsed upon our heads, flapping madly. Then came a brief lull, accompanied by a curious hissing noise, as clouds of ice-particles rained down upon the tent. One of us struggled outside to repair the broken guy-rope and to fasten the others more securely. This operation was barely completed before the next blast was upon us with a noise like a cannonade. Each blast seemed more violent than the last and more prolonged. We lay in our sleeping-bags, braced up against the sides of the tent, each clinging to one of the poles in the hope of relieving the strain on the guy-ropes. It seemed impossible that the tent would not be ripped to pieces, and we fully expected to have to ride out the storm lying in the open in our sleeping-bags. So during the next lull we put on all our sweaters, gloves and balaclava helmets, and put our boots inside our bags. We discovered later that the wind was being deflected by the steep northern flank of the ridge so that its main force was in an upward direction, and was thus not fully concentrated upon the tent. All the same the tent was getting a terrific hammering, and the fact that none of the stitching gave way was a fine tribute to the workmanship that had gone into its construction. Night fell and there was no slackening in the violence of the storm. Each brief lull was accompanied by a shower of ice-dust, each blast by a tremendous booming noise which seemed to shake the whole ridge. So it went on for hour after hour. I did not expect to sleep, and lay with my head buried in my bag with my arms stretched up and my hands clutching the tent-pole. Once it became evident that the tent was not going to be torn to pieces or lifted bodily off the ridge, I began to derive a good deal of enjoyment out of the noise of the storm, which I think was more violent than any I had experienced on Everest. Indeed, the noise seemed to have a soporific effect, which I have often found to be the case with violent thunderstorms, and in spite of the wild jolting of the tent I fell into a desultory sleep.

The storm was still raging at dawn the next morning, but its violence was declining and by eight o'clock we were able to get the Primus going and to cook breakfast. We decided to spend the day climbing the snow-peak on the ridge to the east. By ten o'clock the wind had slackened enough to allow us to start, and before we had been going for an hour it was quite calm. It was a delightful climb. The ridge was long; it was not particularly difficult and the snow was perfect, but it was narrow and heavily corniced so that we had to keep our wits about us. From the top (16,500 feet), the view of Bogdo was really magnificent, while in the other direction the ice-ridge continued over another peak about the same height as our own to another wide col, beyond which stood the massive "Six Thousander." We returned to our camp at four o'clock. We had thought of staying another night there and possibly making our way along the ridge towards Bogdo the next day. But while we were brewing tea the wind started to blow exactly as it had done the previous night, and it soon became clear that it would develop into another storm. We quickly decided that one was enough, and set about packing up the camp. It was nearly six o'clock when we started down, and it was already almost impossible to stand on the crest of the ridge. A few feet down on the lee side the air was still, and as we climbed down we could enjoy to the full the sight of the great golden plumes flying from the tops of the peaks, and the deepening colours of evening. We seemed to be descending into a sea of Mediterranean blue, transparent in the shallows immediately below, opaque beyond. We reached the camp beyond the col the following afternoon.

On the 25th we went down to the Khasak encampment. The Beg had returned. He was a charming old man, extremely friendly and hospitable. The other Khasaks, following his example, warmed to us and we had a very pleasant evening with them. On the 26th we climbed a sharp rock peak, about five thousand feet above the valley. Its corries were filled with small, steep glaciers, and it provided an amusing climb. The day was fine and still. We spent two hours lounging on the summit, from which, as it was quite isolated from the main range, there was a splendid view. Away to the west we saw a score of peaks belonging to the eastern ranges of the Tien Shan, every one of them as spectacular as Bogdo itself. The region is virtually unknown. It would provide a glorious field for exploration and mountaineering.

Soon after we had returned to the encampment that evening, two Tungans turned up. It appeared that they were the owners of all the flocks in the valley, the Khasaks herding them, using the milk and wool and presumably taking some percentage of the profit resulting from the increase in the flocks. It seemed a curious form of capitalism. We had found the same system among the Kirghiz in the Pamirs and Western Tien Shan, where the owners were often Turkis from the plains. But I was even more surprised to find it among the Khasaks who are such a particularly tough and independent people. And how had it survived the numerous civil wars and revolutions of recent decades and the period of Soviet domination over the Province? Surely during those times it would have been easy for the Khasaks to break away from their alien masters and to assume ownership of the flocks themselves, even if in peaceful times they failed to win economic independence. It appeared as though there must be some advantage to the Khasaks in the system, though it is difficult to see where it lay. It was evident that our hosts had no affection for the visitors. The atmosphere in the tent that evening was strained. The previous evening the Khasaks had been gay and talkative, now they were silent and rather morose. The Tungans were an unpleasant-looking pair.

The next day we hired some ponies from the Khasaks and travelled on down the valley. There is no fir forest on the southern side of the range, though lower down, the valleys are filled with thickets of willow and other deciduous trees. We reached the main highway between Turfan and Urumchi, where we had no difficulty in getting a lift on a lorry to the capital.

When we reached Urumchi we found that the new British Consul had arrived, but there was no sign of my Indian successor. It appeared that he could not be expected for several months yet and there was nothing for it but for me to return to Kashgar. But when we went to get the old Ford lorry out of the workshops it was discovered that there was a crack in one of the cylinders which it would take at least a week to repair. There was nothing for me to do in Urumchi during that time. I would have liked to pay a visit to Ili, but that area had been politically separated from the rest of the Province for more than a year and it was virtually impossible to go there. The weather was cloudless. The North-east Ridge of Bogdo stood out against the clear blue sky, a stabbing reminder of our failure even to attempt the only reasonable route to the summit. The ridge would surely by now be clear of winter snow and in perfect condition. Dreesen talked of spending the week-end going up to visit our Khasak friends on the southern side of the mountain. The temptation was too great. In a week we would just have time, if the weather held, to make an attempt on the ridge and get back to Urumchi. On Saturday we set out in the American Consulate lorry, followed the Turfan road for about thirty miles and turned up a rough path leading to the valley we had come down. We managed to get the lorry a long way up. On Sunday, while we were marching up the valley, the weather broke, and for the next three days it snowed heavily on the mountain, though very little rain fell in the valley below. Bill and I, Lhakpa and Agasha went on and camped by the lake in the defile below the big north glacier. A few hundred feet above, the great rock precipices were completely white with the newly fallen snow.

By the morning of the fourth day the weather had cleared a bit, but by then so much snow had fallen on the mountain that it was obvious that it would be impossible to attempt the North-east Ridge for a long time to come, even if the weather remained perfectly fine. However, we wanted to make certain, so we went up the glacier and started to climb the ridge leading to the Small Pointed Peak. As we had expected, even here nearly a foot of new snow covered the rocks. With a good deal of difficulty we reached a point about 15,000 feet, a little way below the High Col. The ridges of the main mountain were festooned with great masses of new snow. There was a great deal of cloud, but for a time after we had reached our highest point it cleared and we had an excellent view of the North-east Ridge. We were a great deal closer to it than ever before. We came to the definite conclusion that in good conditions it could be climbed, and in a single day from the High Col.

I must confess that I had rather hoped we should decide otherwise, for now I knew that we should always think of Bogdo with a slight feeling of regret. If we had planned otherwise than we did, if we had reconnoitred the East Ridge before committing ourselves to it, if we had not wasted so much time in the beginning, we might—indeed, I think we would—have reached the top of that very lovely mountain.

How much of the pleasure of mountaineering lies in all the varied experience of the Attempt; how much depends upon the garnish of Success? It is a philosophical question that most climbers would find hard to answer honestly. We like to think that success is not essential to our maximum enjoyment, which should derive from our knowledge and experience of mountains. The men who eventually reach the top of Everest will not know the mountain as Mallory knew it. Had we in the beginning tried the North-east Ridge and succeeded, we should not have experienced Bogdo as we did. But where is the man whose enjoyment is not slightly shadowed by the memory of failure, particularly when it was due to his fault?

Our greatest compensation came at the end, and there were moments during the next three days when I really believed that I was glad the snow had frustrated this last attempt. We decided that evening to send Agasha down by the way we had come, taking with him the tents, stoves and other surplus baggage, while Bill, Lhakpa and I, carrying only our sleeping-bags and a minimum of food, went westward, keeping as near as possible to the main axis of the range. The journey took us two and a half days. It was one of the most delightful walks I have ever had. In a small way, it had the charm of exploration. It had all the variety that we could have wished.

We started at dawn and climbed in two hours to a little glacier col to the west. From here we looked down into a grassy cwm, half-encircled by ice-mountains, which formed the head of the main valley of the Heavenly Pool. On the floor of the cwm there was a small lake, by the shore of which we saw a herd of about twenty ibex grazing. On the slopes, as in all the upper valleys of the range, there were a great number and variety of alpine flowers. Half a mile below the lake, coming over a grassy mound, we stumbled on another large herd of ibex. They were lying on the ground, the nearest only fifteen yards from us. We crossed above the head of a dark, forested gorge which led down to the Heavenly Pool, and climbed up to a gap in the next ridge running north from the peaks of the main axis. So we went on throughout the day, crossing cols, I forget how many, and keeping close under the long line of ice-peaks. At about five o'clock we halted for the night on a grassy bank by a stream which came from a small glacier. We found plenty of yak dung for a fire. After cooking and eating our supper, we lay in our sleeping-bags and watched the evening colours fade on the peaks until they were black against the stars.

We started again at dawn, climbed up past the shoulder of the last of the ice-peaks and reached the crest of a broad hog's-back which was the westward extension of the axis of the range. Except for a few basalt towers, it was level and delightfully easy to walk along. On either hand, the view was uninterrupted. It was most exhilarating to go for mile after mile along this strange isolated ridge, eight thousand feet above the plains. To the south the mountains of the Tien Shan were clear, their height exaggerated by a wide plain between us and them and by our own height above it. Soon after noon we reached the end of the ridge and found ourselves at the hub of half a dozen deep valleys radiating outwards. Though we were high enough above them to trace the course of each, their tributaries seemed to intermingle in a confusing maze. Each was filled with dense fir forest, which reached to a point some two thousand feet below us. We sat for an hour debating which we should choose, reluctant to descend from our lofty eminence. Then we climbed down a rocky gully, disturbing a covey of ram chikor. The gully became a nullah, filled with brambles and scrub, already tinted with the reds and golds of autumn; the gorge opened into a great valley, sombre under dense fir forest except where the river still sparkled in the sunlight and in the occasional grassy clearings. At one of these, at four o'clock, we stopped for half an hour to drink milk in a Khasak tent. By now there was a wide pathway, with bridges where it crossed the river, and walking became a relaxation. A couple of hours later we began to emerge into the foothills; the fir forest had ceased and we were in a valley filled with willow and briar thickets, flanked by low hills covered with tall grass and scrub. It was very beautiful in the golden evening light, but the river had disappeared underground and the prospect of a waterless, and therefore foodless, night almost spoilt its enchantment. It was nine o'clock and quite dark before we reached another Khasak encampment.

Our hosts were very friendly and, besides plying us with milk and cream and cooking our food, they agreed to lend us three ponies and to send a man to show us the way. We started again as soon as it was light. A tiny path led out of the valley and across an intricate pattern of hills and nullahs, until, after about three hours, we reached open downland. My pony was more energetic than the others or I urged it with more effect, for I got well ahead, travelling at a fast trot and occasionally cantering. Between the rounded downs, the wide fertile valleys cultivated by Tungan farmers were filled with golden wheat. The harvest had just begun. It was beautiful country, but I suppose it was partly the contrast with the scenes of the last two days, in themselves so wonderfully varied, that lent to it a special enchantment. The forested spurs of Bogdo Ola were now far up to the left. The ice-peaks were just coming into view.

CHAPTER XII

CHAKRAGIL; AND HUNZA AGAIN

I ARRIVED back in Kashgar with Tilman on 24th August. Even if I had been able to leave immediately, it was already much too late for us to embark upon the glacier journey from Shimshal to Panamik. As it was, besides having various matters to attend to before handing over my charge, I had to await instructions from the Governments of India and Pakistan, and this would have made our departure too late even for the alternative journey I had planned, that south from Khotan across the Kuen Lun to Leh. Moreover, by that time Ladakh had become a battle-ground, and it seemed likely that we would not be able to travel through. But although we had to abandon these fascinating plans, there was time before the winter set in for one more mountain venture. There was no lack of choice. For my part I favoured either another journey to the Uch Tash country to the north-east or an exploration of the still unknown valleys coming down from the North Face of Kungur. Bill, on the other hand, hankered after climbing a great peak; and none was more attractive than Chakragil. It would have taken too long to get round to the southern side of this mountain which we had seen to be climbable, and as I could not get away immediately, we agreed to a compromise. He would spend a week or ten days reconnoitring the North Ridge of Chakragil and come back to report. If he found a possible route, we would return together to try it; if not, we would go to the Kungur valleys. He set out at the end of August, taking Mersh with him.

I had paid a brief visit to the northern side of Chakragil with my wife in May 1947, when we camped for three days close to the foot of the mountain in a valley of extraordinary beauty. Our camp, at 8,500 feet, was set in a grassy glade surrounded by tall firs. The forested slopes of the valley ended abruptly in bare, sweating precipices of rock, cleft by dark ravines, and surmounted by snowy peaks. Lofty water-falls cascaded down the cliffs; sometimes they were caught by the wind and diffused into waving curtains of spray. There were seven in all, though not all were visible from the camp; some must have been six or seven hundred feet high. The precipices formed a rough frame for the great peaks at the head of the valley. A few hundred yards from our camp was the snout of a glacier, which appeared almost jet-black against the green firs. The glacier was only two or three miles long. Its head lay immediately beneath a cirque, 12,000 feet high, of terraced and fluted ice, which formed the North Face of the two peaks of Chakragil.

A remarkable feature of the glacier was the abnormal size of the ablation valleys at its sides. Standing on one of them, we could see nothing of the glacier, which was screened by the huge grass-covered lateral moraine. This produced the curious illusion that the gigantic ice-precipices of Chakragil rose straight out of the luxuriant grass of the meadows on the floor of the ablation valley. Though it was too early in the year for them to be at their best, there were already masses of wild flowers on the meadows. The fir forest ex-tended a mile or more above the snout of the glacier. Seen from above, the glacier had the curious appearance of being confined in a narrow, built-up trough, running down the centre of a grassy and forested valley.

There was no possibility of climbing that stupendous North Face of the peaks. But running northward from the higher of the two summits there was a great ridge which in its lower reaches formed the western side of the valley we were in. It had seemed to me that if we could get a camp on to the crest of this ridge it would be possible to climb it to the summit of the mountain. I could see no way of reaching the ridge from this side, and I had no time then to explore the opposite side. To do this was now Bill's object.

If we were to attempt to climb Chakragil, which is just over twenty-two thousand feet high, it would greatly increase our chances of success if we had with us a third man to help us to carry the loads to our high camps. Besides this, I am strongly opposed to a party of two climbing for long on crevassed glaciers if it can be avoided, particularly when carrying heavy loads. If one man falls into a bad crevasse so that he is dangling on the rope, it may be extremely difficult, if not impossible, for a single companion to get him out; with a third man to help, the task is a very great deal easier. The problem was, who to take with us. After his two years of comparatively sedentary life in Kashgar, I very much doubted whether Gyalgen was up to it. We had been disappointed with Agasha's performance on Bogdo. I had intended to get hold of my Kirghiz friend, Khurban, and ask him to come with us; he, at least, would be in first-rate physical condition; he was a good climber and used to carrying loads.

While Bill was away, I went for a week-end hunting *ovis poli* in the hills west of Minyol. Lhakpa, Kapak and I were in camp by a spring on the Saturday evening when a party of three Kirghiz turned up. They were on their way to Kashgar from the west and they stopped with us for the night. While we were having supper, one of them, named Mahmud, a small wiry man of thirty or so, asked me if I would like him to come with me the next day. He knew those hills well, he said, and had hunted there himself more than once. I welcomed his suggestion. We set out together an hour before dawn, and had a very long and tiring day. I was tremendously impressed by his skill and agility as a climber and by his stamina; he walked up-hill with beautiful ease of movement, tackled difficult places with a steady confidence which overcame them far more quickly than I could, and by the end of the day seemed to be as fresh as when we had started.

I thought I had found the ideal man to come with us on Chakragil. He was intelligent, quiet and not excitable, and though, of course, he had never climbed on an ice-mountain, he was used to crossing high passes and living among valleys which were snow-covered in winter. I asked him if he would like to come with me for a couple of weeks to the Pamirs, explaining that the object of the trip was to climb one of the great snow-peaks, that he would have to carry a load, and would, of course, be well paid. He jumped at the idea, and the matter was settled without more ado.

Bill arrived back in Kashgar on 8th September. He was, for Bill, unusually excited. He had been into the South-western Cwm of Chakragil and was fairly confident that he had found a way of climbing on to the crest of the North Ridge. He could not be certain, for while in the cwm he had struck a patch of bad weather and the intermittent views that he had had of the surrounding mountains had left him so confused about the topography of the region that he was not even sure that he had identified Chakragil. Nor had he been able to see enough of the North Ridge to confirm my opinion of it.

As I was still expecting telegraphic instructions from the Governments of India and Pakistan about the future of the Consulate, which might require a fairly prompt reply, I did not feel justified in being away for very long. However, if necessary a messenger could be sent to fetch me back, and with that proviso I decided to allow myself a clear ten days, which, if the weather was kind, should give us time to attempt the peak. Taking with us Gyalgen, Mahmud and two Turkis, from whom we had hired pack-ponies, we started on 10th September and that evening reached Tash-malik, a large oasis at the southern edge of the plains.

From Tashmalik our way led for about ten miles up the valley of the Gez River. The hills on either side of this, like all the foot-hills surrounding the Tarim Basin, were utterly barren, their weird conglomerate cliffs and arid nullahs in stark contrast to the miles of green oasis we had just left; that contrast which is the most characteristic scenic feature of Southern Sinkiang. The morning was clear, and the great snowy mass of Kungur now towered above us. The fluted ice-ridges of Chakragil looked glorious against the blue sky. The river was still in its summer spate, but here it flowed over a mile-wide bed, and was split into several channels. Even so, the current was so strong that it took us an hour to find places where the ponies could ford them. Before the Gez Valley was swallowed up in its great gorge, we turned to the westward, up the first large tributary, which was called Oui Tagh Jilga. This, too, was arid, except for stretches of tamarisk and briar jungle along the banks of the river. Some six miles up-stream the river had cut its way through a high barrier of conglomerate rock, which had been eroded into an extraordinary convolution of clean-cut ridges and canyons, very like those of the Tushuk Tagh Range, only on a smaller scale. Past this barrier we came to a wide stretch of cultivation surrounding the scattered village of Oui Tagh Aghiz. The land here had clearly been formed by the sedimentary deposits from a large lake, which had been dammed back by the conglomerate barrier before the river cut its way through to its present level. Stepping round the last corner of the defile, as through a doorway, the green fields and orchards presented a lovely and unexpected sight. When I had come here before, the fruit blossom had been out and the fields of young corn had been fringed with wide borders of wild iris.

On the third day we marched on up the Oui Tagh Jilga, past the entrance of the valley leading up to the North Face of Chakragil, and that afternoon we reached a group of *akois* set among the first of the fir trees near the snout of a glacier. We were warmly greeted by the inhabitants, with whom Bill had already made friends and whose manifold ills, real and imaginary, had been treated, apparently successfully, by the Doctor. After the usual feast of curds and cream, we went on, accompanied by a number of the local Kirghiz. We followed a steep path through the forest and eventually reached a wide grassy shelf, a couple of miles long, formed by an ancient lateral moraine and its attendant ablation valley. The shelf was used by the Kirghiz as a summer grazing-ground, and some *akois* were still there. It overlooked a great "concordia" of glaciers, which flowed down from a vast cirque of lofty mountains. Chakragil itself, tucked away in the left-hand corner of the cirque, was hidden behind a great rock peak, which Bill had named "Geometry Peak" from the extraordinary sharpness of the angles formed by its ridges. Several peaks of the cirque I recognized as forming part of the great panorama visible from Kashgar. From there, their forms had become so familiar to me, like part of the background pattern of a well-known picture, that it seemed strange to see them so close, the intricate detail of their structure, hitherto invisible, now dominating the scene.

The two aneroid barometers which Bill had brought from England had both been broken. But among the miscellaneous survey instruments left behind at the Consulate, I imagine by Sir Aurel Stein or perhaps by one of my predecessors with geographical tastes, were two hypsometers, or boiling-point thermometers. We had brought one of these with us. The solemnity of its use, setting it up, lighting the little spirit-lamp and waiting until it puffed like a toy steam-engine, lent a pleasant air of old-fashioned dignity to our expedition, and of course greatly entertained our hosts in the *akoi* that evening. It informed us that we were just over ten thousand feet above sea-level.

Bill, Gyalgen, Mahmud and I started early next morning, taking with us two tents and provisions for about four days. The two pack-ponies, in charge of one of the Turkis, carried the loads to the farther end of the two-mile terrace and a little beyond, until the ground became too broken for them to come any farther. Thereafter we shouldered the loads ourselves, and plodded on at a leisurely pace.

CHAKRAGIL : NORTH FACE

TRAVELLING THROUGH HUNZA

I always dislike intensely the idea of carrying a load, particularly when I am out of practice, as one always is on a short mountaineering expedition, and I always try as far as I decently can to avoid it. But when circumstances make it unavoidable, I am always mildly surprised that the misery involved is so much less than I expected. In some situations it is always unpleasant; one is over flat country, but then I dislike walking over flat country even without a load, and fortunately I have rarely had to do so with one; another is in difficult jungle when you have to twist your body about and you cannot develop a rhythmic action. But under favourable conditions I even derive a certain sombre satisfaction from this form of toil; it is impossible to hurry, and impatience has to be subdued; one is forced to pay strict attention to that really very fascinating art of walking up-hill, the main features of which are controlled and balanced movement and careful choosing of foot-hold; and, perhaps best of all, one has an excuse for frequent halts to admire the view. So it was to-day, and though the going was not easy, we managed, unless our hypsometer lied, to climb four thousand feet with remarkably little discomfort.

When we left the ponies, we were close to the huge rock precipices of Geometry Peak, which towered some six thousand feet above us. A broken ice-fall on the glacier to our right forced us to climb diagonally up a great cone of debris at the foot of the cliffs. Deep grooves in its surface and large blocks of ice at its base provided evidence that a recent avalanche had added to the cone, and I was very relieved when, after about three-quarters of an hour, we reached a little rock terrace above and beyond. From here, for several hours we were confined to a dirty trough between the glacier and the flanking mountain-side; the former was much too broken to afford a passage, while the latter was composed of steep, loose scree. On the whole it was not hard going in the trough, though from time to time little cliffs of ice barred the way and provided some difficulty. At about noon we reached a corner, beyond which the ice receded from the mountain-side and there was greater freedom of movement. We stopped here for lunch and then climbed some two thousand feet up a wide gully, which led us to the crest of a broad scree-covered ridge overlooking the upper basin of the glacier. This was the farthest point that Bill had reached a week or so before. There was a spring of water close at hand and we decided to pitch our first camp here.

The weather, which had been cloudy and threatening the day before, had cleared and the evening was fine. Our camp on the ridge commanded a splendid view of all the peaks of the great cirque and of the basin of ice that it enclosed. Across a wide glacier immediately below us, the North-west Face of Chakragil rose in a series of long ice-terraces or hanging glaciers to the summit dome. To the left, completing the cirque in that direction and ending apparently in the great precipices of Geometry Peak, was the North Ridge. There appeared to be two possible ways of reaching it. One was along a steep and narrow corridor running up from the floor of the glacier between the face of Chakragil and an impenetrable jumble of ice-cliffs to the left. Although in places it was badly crevassed, this corridor looked tempting but for the fact that it ran immediately below the hanging glaciers of Chakragil and was thus menaced by ice-avalanches. Alternatively, in a direct line with the ridge we were on, there appeared to be an easy route past the ice-cliffs to their left; but from where we stood we could not see the lower part of it. So while the rest of us were pitching camp, Bill went on up the ridge to reconnoitre. He returned an hour later and reported that a narrow neck of ice connected the top of our ridge with the snow-slopes which we could see beyond. This was a great relief, for I had been contemplating the route up the corridor and had come to the conclusion that it would involve our spending too long a time

under fire from the hanging glaciers for the risk to be justi-
fiable.

While supper was cooking, we boiled our hypsometer. We
discovered that, not unnaturally, the thermometer gave the
same reading when immersed in boiling tea-water as in the
ingenious little steam-engine provided by the makers, so we
decided to lighten our loads by the weight of the latter. We
would take for granted the height of the summit, where we
would not be brewing tea. Our altitude worked out at
14,000 feet. We estimated that the crest of the North Ridge
at the point where we would reach it was about three
thousand feet above us. Providing the going was good, we
could reasonably expect to carry a camp to there the next
day. A final camp on the face of the mountain at about
nineteen thousand five hundred feet should put us within
easy reach of the summit, even if the snow conditions were
much worse than we had reason to expect. Mahmud had
gone quite well that day, and had made no complaint about
his load, though I suspect that Gyalgen had seen to it that
he carried the heaviest. He did not seem to be in the least
daunted by the prospect of climbing this great ice-mountain,
or of camping on its lofty ridges. To test him, I suggested
that he should change places with Gyalgen and remain
below; but he would not hear of it, and was evidently determined to win the rich reward I had offered him if we succeeded in reaching the top. The cloudless sky and the pink
glow which filled the cirque at sunset gave promise of fine
weather. We settled down for the night with high hopes.

We started at six o'clock the next morning, leaving behind
one of the tents, Gyalgen's bedding and some food. Gyalgen
came with us carrying a load as far as he could safely return
alone; after which, he would go right down to the *akois*,
taking with him the things we had left behind.

I always find that the events of a day spent in carrying a
high camp up a mountain tend in retrospect to become
telescoped in such a manner that it becomes difficult to dis-

tinguish them in their true perspective, and still harder to understand how the whole business took so long. In normal life, nine hours spent upon a single job seems to me a very long time (this may be because with me it so rarely occurs). But in this matter of carrying high camps, although individual hours may drag, at some point in the day, time seems to run together so that three o'clock, the hour at which one generally starts looking around for a suitable place to put the camp, suddenly appears out of a confused series of contrasting emotions. For the first hour I plod along in a mood of deep gloom, of self-pity and of dislike both for my companions and for the whole silly business of mountain climbing. I am stiff and tired, my legs and shoulders ache, in my hands and feet I detect undeniable symptoms of frost-bite, the slopes above look impossibly long and steep, and my only desire is to lie down and sleep. The first halt works a subtle but profound change, and during the next spell, though it would be overstating the case to say that I am happy, I am not wholly insensitive to the grandeur of my surroundings, I am tolerant at least towards the minor short-comings of my friends and willing to admit that mountain-eering is not entirely unrewarding. Thereafter I swing between these emotional extremes. The quality of the snow, the moisture of my throat and the apparent progress of the party are among the factors motivating this change of mood; but there are evidently many others which escape the keenest introspection.

To begin with, on this day, all went very well. It was freezing hard and it would be several hours before the sun climbed above the North Ridge and started to soften the snow. The neck of ice at the top of our rock ridge carried us comfortably over a nasty ice-fall. The slopes beyond were in excellent condition. Mahmud seemed to be going rather slowly, but we evidently did not take this seriously enough to change our plans. It must have been about eleven o'clock and we had just hauled our baggage up the steep upper lip of a crevasse, when we decided that it was time for Gyalgen to leave us. We watched him down to easy ground, distributed his load amongst us and started on. Less than an hour later Mahmud began to show signs of distress. As the snow was beginning to get soft and Bill and I took it in turns to kick the steps, and as, too, we were having a little trouble in finding a way through the crevasses and small ice-cliffs which barred the way, the pace was in any case very slow, and he had plenty of time to rest. Even so, at about half-past one it became evident that he could not carry his load any farther. We relieved him of it, and while one of us was kicking the steps the other carried it up in relays. In spite of the delay, we had made such good progress that by three o'clock we reached a little hollow only fifty feet below the crest of the North Ridge. It was a snug little place, the bottom of a shallow crevasse, sheltered from the wind on three sides by ice-cliffs. We set to work to make camp, light the Primus and melt ice for tea.

Mahmud's collapse was a bitter blow. We had found a beautiful solution to the cardinal problem of reaching the North Ridge. The altitude of our camp turned out to be 17,500 feet, which was even higher than we had hoped to reach that day. A very moderate carry the next day would have placed us within easy reach of the summit, now only some four thousand five hundred feet above us. We still hoped that Mahmud might recover with a night's rest. But from the first the prospect was not very encouraging. He refused to eat anything, vomited frequently and in the intervals lay groaning on the floor of the tent. I was terribly sorry for him, but I could not help bemoaning the fact that if he had told us only an hour sooner that he was feeling ill, we could have sent him down with Gyalgen and gone on by ourselves.

We ate our evening meal, and then, oppressed by that strange, ethereal loneliness which settles upon a high camp at evening, we arranged ourselves as best we could for a

long, uncomfortable night. At sunset a westerly wind started
to blow with considerable force. In spite of our sheltered
position, the noise of flapping canvas and of drift snow beating against the tent made sleep difficult. With three in a tent
designed for two our space was cramped. For a long time I
lay brooding, in that futile, restless way that one does at
night, upon our situation. Unless Mahmud made an unexpected recovery, it seemed that we had two courses open
to us. We could attempt to reach the summit from this camp;
but we were not acclimatized to this altitude, and unless the
snow were in excellent condition all the way we were hardly
likely to succeed. The alternative was to take Mahmud down
and return later; but we would probably have to take him
down the whole 7,500 feet to the *akois,* and in that case we
could not get back here for another three days, even if the
weather held. It was already very late in the year and a heavy
fall of snow would make even the North Ridge inaccessible.
This, of course, was a potent reason for not staying on the
mountain with a sick man. Of course, if Mahmud showed
any sign of improvement by the morning, assuming that he
was suffering from altitude, we might stay where we were
for a day in the hope that on the following day he might be
well enough to come up another couple of thousand feet with
us, even without a load; for, clearly, we could neither leave
him here without a tent nor go up ourselves without one.

These depressing speculations continued to revolve monotonously in my mind, while, in the brief lulls in the
windstorm, I could hear poor Mahmud groaning and sometimes vomiting. He spent most of the night crouched on his
hands and knees, whether in prayer or to relieve his sickness
I could not tell. Though I slept a little, the night seemed
interminable, and I have rarely been more glad to see the
dawn. The wind dropped and the sun rose into a cloudless
sky. While we were brewing tea, Bill and I discussed the
situation. We agreed that before deciding anything we would
go out for a breath of fresh air. A small mountain tent is a

bad place for making decisions, for in it one's mind seems to become as cramped as one's body.

We roped up and climbed on to the crest of the North Ridge. We had grown accustomed to the panorama of the great glacier cirque to the west; fine though it was, it was nothing to the scene that now opened before us on the eastern side of the ridge. It was not a view of distance, for the plains to the north were misty and featureless and the mountains of the Kungur massif were hidden behind the eastern peak of Chakragil. It was the nearer objects and their peculiar arrangement that held us entranced. We looked straight down nine thousand feet, with nothing visible of the intervening precipice, to the grassy alps and the dark fir forest surrounding them, where my wife and I had camped some eighteen months before. They were still in shadow, but the air was very clear and as our eyes became accustomed to the gloom we could see tiny wreaths of smoke rising from the Kirghiz encampments. The *akois* themselves were invisible. To the right, suspended above this great abyss, close at hand and dazzling in the early morning sun, were the hanging glacier terraces, tier upon tier of them, supported by scores of slender buttresses of fluted ice, which formed the North Face of Chakragil. Two-thirds of this mighty precipice was now below us. The effect of depth, enhanced as it was by the delicately balanced poise of the vast and complex structure, was overwhelming. Beyond the topmost terrace we could see into a deep recess, a peaceful glen, which nestled beneath the mile-long ridge between the twin summits, its walls and floor forming a perfect curve of unbroken snow.

The crest of the North Ridge, though heavily corniced upon its eastern side, was broad enough to allow us to walk comfortably along it. It mounted at a gentle gradient and, some two thousand feet above us, merged into the great ice-dome of Chakragil. The climb would have presented not the slightest technical difficulty. We made our way along the ridge, partly to test the snow and partly to see the fantastic view to the east from a new angle. Our feet sank about nine inches into the snow. Even if this became no worse higher up, it would probably have made our progress too slow to reach the summit in a single day. But with another camp even fifteen hundred feet higher, we could hardly have failed to do so, providing the weather held for another thirty hours. But before we had left the camp we had little doubt that Mahmud would be able to go no farther, and we had almost resigned ourselves to the bitter disappointment of having to abandon our project when the summit was almost within our grasp. We stayed a while to gaze at what was in many ways the finest piece of mountain scenery I have ever seen. Then we returned to camp.

When we got back we found poor Mahmud still lying in the tent. We got him out and found that his condition was even worse than we had thought. He seemed scarcely able to stand; he was still vomiting frequently, and we now noticed that when he coughed, blood appeared on his lips. There was now no question but that we must get him down as soon as possible. Indeed, I felt profound relief that only one course was open to us; for I know of few more difficult decisions than those involving a choice between pressing and abandoning an attempt upon a mountain when the latter course is not absolutely necessary. We packed up our things and, leaving behind most of the food and the tin of kerosene, made them into two loads. Then we roped up and started down. Mahmud staggered to the edge of the hollow and collapsed. There was nothing we could do but to tow him along, which was not difficult for us, but must have been extremely unpleasant for him, for he often gathered momentum and slid or rolled past us and had to be pulled up at the end of the rope. Over the steep places we lowered him as gently as we could. He thought he was dying and asked us to leave him where he was. Once, when we halted for a long rest, he asked me for a pencil and paper and pro ceeded to write a brief letter which he asked me to deliver to his family when I got back.

Eventually we got him down to the head of the ridge on which we had camped two days before, by which time he had so far recovered as to be able to walk for short spells by supporting himself on our shoulders. I was convinced that he was suffering from nothing more serious than altitude sickness. This was confirmed, both by his quick recovery when we got down to lower levels and, when we got back to Kashgar, by a thorough examination by the Doctor, who could find nothing wrong with him. It was certainly the most severe attack of altitude sickness that I have ever witnessed. That the victim should have been a youngish man, so particularly tough and strong, who had spent all his life among mountains was certainly remarkable. But I have long ceased to wonder at unaccountable manifestations of this capricious complaint.

On the evening of the following day, the weather showed unmistakable signs of a change for the worse. Our Kirghiz hosts told us that this was the beginning of the first autumn snowfalls, and announced their intention of moving down to lower pastures. They showed us an interesting pass to the north of the glacier cirque, and two of them were kind enough to accompany us to its summit. It led us into a long valley running northward to Yolchi Moinak, which we had passed on our way back from Mustagh Ata the previous year. From there, we travelled again across the thirty-mile stretch of desert to Opal, and thence back to Kashgar.

We had reason, I think, to attribute our failure to reach the summit of Chakragil to ill luck. But for all that, we had shown a singular lack of imagination in devising our plan. It would have been far better if Bill had taken Gyalgen with him on his first trip, with the understanding that if he failed to find a route he would meet me ten days later—say, at the mouth of the Oui Tagh River—while if I did not find him there, I would come on up to the glacier cirque. Of course, we did not know of the existence of this at the time, but we could hardly have failed to meet. This would have given them more than a week's training at climbing to high altitudes, which would probably have been sufficient to enable Gyalgen to recover enough of his form to come with us on the mountain. They could have employed at least some of their time carrying loads up the lower part of the mountain, which incidentally would have been very nice for me! Perhaps this is being wise after the event, but I have a feeling that in the 'thirties we would have exercised more forethought.

We got back to Kashgar on 21st September. Bill had decided, instead of travelling via Hunza and Gilgit, to go westward from Misgar across the Chillinji Pass to Ishkumen and thence to Chitral. I would have liked very much to go with him on this journey, but two considerations prevented this. First, I could not get away until 10th October, and every week that he delayed lessened his chances of getting across the high passes on his route; secondly, I was anxious to visit the Mir of Hunza, with whom I had various matters to discuss. So we decided to go our separate ways and, if possible, to meet in Chitral before the end of November. He left Kashgar on 29th September.

As the day of my departure approached, I spent much time in sentimental reflection. During my years in Kashgar I had been accustomed each morning to ride ten or twelve miles before breakfast. Now I went over each of my half-dozen rides in turn, giving full rein to the exquisite nostalgia that each intimate landmark induced: the mill in the willow grove across the valley, where the boy used to blow his horn to announce that the miller was ready for fresh supplies of grain; the wide, green river-flats of Sogaluk, where in winter wild duck used to congregate in their thousands and where, on a frosty morning, the steam would rise from a hundred ice-girt pools into the early sunlight; the little grassy glade, down which I used to gallop at full speed, usually with thoughts of breakfast uppermost in my mind; the high loess bluff, where, on clear mornings, I would rein my pony and watch the sunrise on the Pamirs. It was all so familiar that it seemed incredible that I would never see any of it again; or, indeed, anything remotely like it, for I believe the countryside of South Sinkiang is unique. Three or four times during those last few days the mountains were clear and, looking at them, I was oppressed by regret for the number of things I had hoped to do and had not done. This was unreasonable, of course, for, although no doubt I had missed opportunities, even if I had had no duties to perform in Kashgar and had been able to give all my time to travel, I could not have covered the whole of that vast field.

I am still amazed at the great good fortune that gave me the chance to know something of Sinkiang and, having watched the recent turn of events, I shudder to think of the narrow margin by which I got that chance. For the Iron Curtain has already clanged down behind me, and it may be many decades before a Western traveller is free to travel there again. What, I wonder, will he find?

My sorrow at leaving Kashgar was softened by the prospect of another six weeks' trek through the Pamirs, the Karakoram and the Hindu Kush. Apart from the break that it meant, I looked forward to this with the keenest pleasure. There are some aspects of a straightforward journey, providing it is done under the right conditions, that are more enjoyable than travelling through unknown country; just as there is delight to be found in climbing a well-known peak behind a guide, pleasure of a kind often lacking in the ascent of an unclimbed mountain. One is pleasantly free from the responsibility of finding the way, and of such tiresome decisions as to whether and when to turn back, how far to press forward each day and whether food and fuel supplies will last. Time and distance, because they are pre-ordained, cease to be matters of importance. One can relax into an untroubled absorption with the changing scenery, with the sheer delight of movement, with the satisfaction of food and rest.

As travelling companions I had Fateh Ali Khan, a Hunza who was in charge of our diplomatic courier service across the passes, and his three sons, while Lhakpa came with me as far as Misgar. Early in October we received word that the water in the Gez River was already low enough to allow the passage of caravans through the great defile between Kungur and Chakragil. So on the 10th, after a farewell party arranged by my staff in camp on the south bank of the Yamen Yar, we set out again for Tashmalik, where for the last time I saw the oases of the Tarim Basin. I had never travelled by the Gez route, and after we had passed the junction of the Oui Tagh Jilga, the way for the next two and a half days, along the bottom of that fantastic gorge, was new to me. The weather was rather bad and we saw little of the great ice-peaks that soared into the clouds above our heads It was slow-going over the rocky floor of the gorge, and we had to ford the river dozens of times as it swung from side to side. In bays, long abandoned by the river, there were extensive jungles of willow and tamarisk; these provided delightful camp-sites, with abundant fuel for large camp-fires.

Beyond the gorge, we joined the route by which we had returned from Mustagh Ata the previous year, and for the next week or so we travelled through the typical Pamir country of wide, rounded river valleys, great stretches of grass land, lakes and ice-mountains. It was perfect country to ride through on a good pony, for over most of the way the surface was good enough to permit cantering. The pack-animal could not do more than twenty-five or thirty miles a day. could cover this distance easily in three hours' riding, and th rest of the time I was free to spend as I chose; to idle in som pleasant spot on the way, to climb to a neighbouring hill-top and sit there for an hour or two, or to stop at a Kirghiz en campment for a bowl of milk. In the mornings, when we started, it was freezing hard, but when the sun had reached us it became pleasantly warm, though never too hot.

From the memory of days so crowded with movement and delight it is difficult to choose the high-lights; for each enchanting moment was really inseparable from the whole, as is the breeze or the smell of heather from a Highland scene. At first, the mighty glaciers of the Kungur Range dominated the landscape. At Kara Kul I lay for four hours on a green meadow by the shore, the white shape of Muztagh Ata mirrored on the calm surface of the lake. At Subashi we stayed the night with our friends from Yam-bulak, and that evening while supper was being cooked I came out of their *akoi* for a stroll. The milking was nearly finished, and the sheep and goats clustered round the tents in their hundreds. In the valley it was already dusk, but across the river the huge snow-dome of the mountain, aflame in the light of the setting sun, was like molten metal against a dark-blue sky. Beyond the Ulugh Robat Pass, near one of the villages in the green Taghama Valley, we met a Kirghiz wedding procession and were invited to the wedding feast.

For five days the weather was fine, but as we reached the southern end of the Taghdumbash Pamir it broke, and beyond Dafdar we marched through a heavy and prolonged snowstorm. The little valley above Lupgaz, when we reached it, was deep in snow, so my last night in Sinkiang was spent in a bleak, cold camp. The next morning was clear again and the great peaks beyond the Mintaka Pass looked magnificent. The ponies had a struggle to get across the Pass in the new snow, but we had started early and by evening we reached a delightful grove of trees several miles below the glacier.

Then followed the part of the journey to which I had been looking forward most. I had never travelled through the Hunza Valley when the autumn colouring was at its best. I was afraid that I might now be too late; but, in fact, I had timed it to perfection. At first, where the tiny hamlets boasted only a few dozen apricots and poplars, the vivid patches of gold and red were small and comparatively rare; though, coming upon them suddenly round the corner of a desolate gorge or perched high up on a vertical precipice, they were striking enough. But after two or three days, when we had travelled down to the more extensive villages, they gradually became a major part of the scene.

Ever since I first saw it in 1937, I have thought of the Hunza Valley as the ultimate manifestation of mountain grandeur. It was now eight years since I had been there and I found to my surprise that my memory had belittled rather than exaggerated its magnificence. I realized, I think, for the first time, how impossible it was to achieve anything like a full imaginative grasp of that country in a few days or weeks; but the realization was exhilarating, not overpowering. My heightened appreciation was due in part to the sudden change from the relatively gentle Pamir scenery we had just left, but in a large measure, too, to the exquisite loveliness of those autumn villages. For never do mountain forms show to such advantage as when they are set in contrast to beauty of another kind.

At five o'clock one evening I emerged from that long canyon where the Hunza River makes a right-angled sweep below Atabad. Baltit came suddenly into view: forty square miles of flaming red and gold, rising in terraces from the river to the base of the rock walls of the twenty-four thousand-foot Kanjut Peaks. In the distance down the valley Rakaposhi stood serene and clear.

INDEX

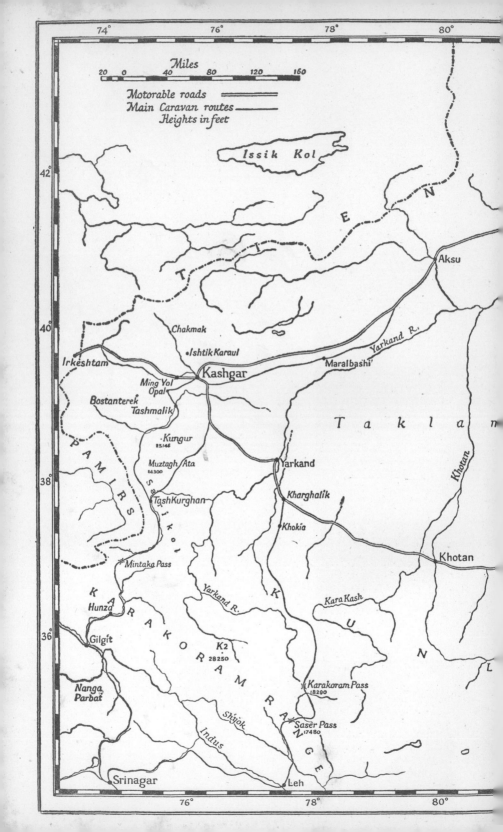